21 inspirational women share
stories with author **Julia Greg**
and photographer **Alex Powna...**

Crossing
Borders

Alex Pownall

Julia Gregson

GRAFFEG

Contents

80

Andrea McLean
Mapping Artist

112

Elizabeth Haycox
Richard Booth's
Bookshop, Café & Cinema

144

Mary Rose Young
Ceramicist & Potter

88

Revel Guest
Film Director & Chair
of Hay Festival

120

Jenny McLoughlin
Paralympic Sprinter

152

Marian Voyce
Butcher

96

Kate Beavan
Farmer & Rural Skills
Teacher

128

Bettina Reeves
Stage Designer &
Puppet Maker

160

Annica Neumuller
Abstract Painter

104

Ineke Berlyn
Textile Artist & Writer

136

Tiffany Murray
Novelist & Lecturer

Glenda Stoneman
Alpaca Breeder

Julia Gregson

Author Julia Gregson was a journalist for 25 years, for Rolling Stone, The Times, Good Housekeeping and The Sydney Morning Herald.

Her first short story won the Literary Review/Rymans award.

Her second novel, East of the Sun was a Sunday Times Best Seller, and Richard and Judy Book Club choice. It won the Romantic Novel of the Year Award, and The Prince Maurice Prize for Literary Love Stories and sold in 25 countries.
Her third novel Jasmine Nights, published by Orion in 2013, was also a Richard and Judy Book Club choice. Married, with one daughter and four step-children, she lives in Whitebrook, on the banks of the Wye, and is working on her fourth novel.

Alex Pownall

Alex Pownall lives in the hilltop village of St.Briavels above the Wye Valley, close to the Welsh border, where she has a darkroom and studio. With an M.A. in Documentary Photography, Newport, and B.A. in Documentary Film, she works as a freelance photographer.

Her exhibitions throughout England and Wales include many local themes: *From the Source to the Estuary* – Bridges of the Wye Valley; *Ebb and Flow* – Lydney Docks & Severn Estuary; *An Alternative Elgar Route* – Places of Inspiration throughout Hereford and Worcester.

Her current exhibition, with a fellow photographer, *Natural Forms: Estuary & Forest*, is accompanied by a book.

Alex's portrait work includes commissions from writers, musicians, and actors for Spotlight. She has two daughters, and is married to playwright and novelist, David Pownall, with whom she has a son.

Introduction

'Welcome to the Graveyard of Ambition,' one neighbour said with gloomy relish when we first moved to the Wye valley thirty years ago, adding, 'particularly for women.'

That wiped the smiles off our faces.

It fed an unspoken fear I had about moving to the country, that away from all the exciting anxieties of the city, I might not, as a freelancer, be able to get work, or might find myself sliding day by day into the gentler pleasures, of say jam-making or bell-ringing.

It's a version of the country which assumes that a metropolis is where you find work, and the country is where you don't. And that you either have to be one thing or another: a fully paid up member of the rat race, or dropped from some exciting club.

And it's not true. It took only a few months of living here to discover that behind hedges, up dirt tracks, in little cottages tucked in the woods, the Wye valley is a hive of industry for the many women who work here.

When Alex and I decided to find out how they made it work, we planned initially to try to cover the whole length of the Wye, which runs from mid-Wales, crosses the English Welsh border at Hay-on-Wye, and flows past Monmouth and Chepstow into the Severn estuary.

This proved impossible. Less than an hour from our homes we found an embarrassment of subjects : a barrister, artists, economists, an opera singer, teachers, a female butcher, theatre designers, a circus owner. We didn't set out to cover all occupations. Also impossible. Or to write a self-help book.

We simply wanted to report on the lives of 21 women.

We called it Crossing Borders, because so many of them seemed to have reached a point of change, or crossed some personal Rubicon, in order to find the job they loved. Some of these crossings were traumatic, some simply a question of having moved, or discovered they had started off in the wrong job. All of these women were refreshingly honest about the times when a happy work and life balance was not possible. Their lives were as untidy and unpredictable as anybody elses.

After visiting them at their places of work: circus big tops, magic gardens, studios, lambing sheds, police headquarters, to name but a few, Alex and I had some interesting conversations on the way home.

We noted that many of our subjects were the daughters of farmers, policemen, airmen, factory workers. Many had gone to comprehensive schools, and with few exceptions found work through trial and error.

A surprising number had found their strengths after shocking reversals of fortune. Elizabeth Haycox, owner of Richard Booth's Bookshop in Hay-on-Wye was widowed with awful suddenness, aged 43. Racehorse trainer, Venetia Williams, was all set to be a jockey until a near fatal fall changed the course of her life.

What linked them all was a sense of how integral to their daily routines the hills, valleys and rivers around them had become. Before picking up a paintbrush, the Ledbury artist, Andrea McLean, walks for two hours every morning in the hills above her house. Mezzo soprano

Catherine King runs for an hour most days to keep herself fit for singing. Venetia Williams is out on her gallops next to the Wye every morning.

And age? Well, that was fascinating too. Some of our women were years past retirement age and still firing on all cylinders. Jean Miller, 83, discovered she was an artist at 63. 'Today,' she says, 'there is no Saturday, and no Sunday.' She is too busy producing the work for her sellout exhibitions.

Revel Guest, the 81-year-old producer of Steven Spielberg's War Horse, will this year produce opera and documentaries, as well as being Chair of the Hay Festival. Her house is invisible from the road, in a remote spot overlooking the River Wye.

We hope you enjoy reading about our 21 as much as we've enjoyed writing and

photographing them. A modest hope too, that if you know a school leaver in despair about their prospects, they'll read this book as a source of inspiration.

That's what it felt like to us.

Julia Gregson

Catherine King

**I ALWAYS HAVE A
'TO DO' LIST AS
LONG AS YOUR ARM**

Imagine this: your much loved father, a vicar, is gravely ill. In a week's time you will sing at Llandaff Cathedral in Cardiff, in Edward Elgar's choral masterpiece, The Dream of Gerontius. Your role is the mezzo soprano angel, who leads a pious man through deathbed agonies and into the afterworld. It's a work of shattering power and beauty, and when we arrived at Catherine King's house at two o'clock on a wet afternoon, she is singing on her own. When she hears our car, she stops. Practice is for her a private thing, but later, when she is persuaded to sing a few bars, it's a heart stopping moment, in which tenderness, prayer, artistry combine in a message of love and farewell.

Catherine King lives in a 500-year-old cottage and converted barn in Llangrove, with sensational views. When they bought the barn 'for peanuts' eighteen years ago, it was 'in little pieces like a jigsaw puzzle'. Fortunately, King's husband, Charles, is a carpenter and a boat builder. He carved the asymmetrical staircase, made the kitchen cabinets, and much of the furniture. The effect is quirky, warm and original. When Catherine was allowed to make one joint in the kitchen, she proudly wrote Chippie's Wife's Joint around it.

The wearing of many hats is for King, an essential part of life here. She is a busy solo artist, and a member of Gothic Voices, a group of four unaccompanied voices who have many recordings to their name and who perform medieval music all over Europe, recently in the roman ruins of Rome, Santiago in Spain.

In appearance, King, with her long limbs and model girl figure is the antithesis of the large-bosomed opera diva. She runs most days in the hills and valleys behind her house, and has Pilates sessions in Goodrich village Hall, essential she says, for letting off steam and maintaining the core strength that aids singing.

Her passion for music began as a member of the choir in her father's church, where she sang solos. A choral scholarship to Cambridge followed, and then a place at the Guildhall School of Music in London, with a teacher's training qualification as back up.

Her packed schedule is filled weeks, months, years ahead. Highlights of last year included a tour with Gothic Voices, the complete Ring Cycle at the Longborough Festival to celebrate Wagner's 200th anniversary year, which garnered national rave reviews, a contemporary oratorio by Kleiberg, Requiem for the Victims of Nazi Persecution, and a UK premier for the Brighton Fringe Festival, 'an incredibly powerful and moving piece'. Her face lights up remembering one unexpected artistic high at a small musical festival in Crickhowell underneath the Brecon Beacons.

A PLACE WHERE YOU HAVE THE TIME AND THE SPACE TO SOAR

AND BE THE CHIPPIE'S WIFE

'It was in May, a beautiful day, in a local church, St Edmunds. The orchestra was an ad-hoc mixture of professionals, playing baroque instruments. The musical director, Stephen Marshall, is great. He never dumbs this festival down, always chooses interesting pieces, and I was part way through a very complex and athletic aria by Galuppi, when I suddenly thought, I'm singing my best ever.'

No question, says Catherine, she would have had a different life in London, perhaps a different career. What draws her back to the Borders is 'the variety of people who live around here: potters, musicians, artists, there are two professional singers living in this valley alone', plus the ballast of it being a down to earth place too. A place where you have the time and the space to soar, and be the Chippie's wife.

My day

'I get up very early at six-thirty, and have breakfast with my son, Duncan who bikes to school in Ross-on-Wye via the back lanes. A leisurely coffee, then normal domestic things: washing, tidying, cooking, followed by admin for concerts, travel arrangements. I always have a 'to do' list as long as your arm.

I'm much better if I get my singing done early in the day, so then it's warm up exercises, scales, vocal massage. I'm usually learning various pieces of music. Right now it's Handel's Israel in Egypt, to be performed near the Arctic Circle in Norway; and Wagner's Wesendonck Lieder – songs for mezzo soprano and orchestra. If I'm performing, I might practise every day, but the vocal chords are like an athlete's muscles, and it's always a delicate balance between straining the muscles and not doing enough.

After practice, I do a run, or I might go to Pilates. I'm a keen runner: I've done an eighteen-mile run in the Beacons, in training for a two-day Mountain Marathon in the Highlands. Next, grab lunch, listen to the Archers, my soap fix for the day, maybe in the afternoon some teaching.

It's not an easy life sometimes – juggling everything – career, husband, house, children, although they're getting easier. My daughter Rowan is now studying French and Linguistics at Oxford. But it's the life I wanted. I knew it was going to be hard, and it is, and I wouldn't do anything else.'

Anne Wareham

LANDSCAPE GARDENER & WRITER

**I STILL DON'T
KNOW WHY IN
THE HELL I DO
THE GARDENING**

Anne Wareham hates gardening.

She hates planting bulbs ('I wasn't made with a hinge in my back'), she hates weeding and stays in bed until 12 o'clock most mornings in order to avoid being disturbed from her main business which is writing. But somehow or other, the author of The Bad Tempered Gardener, gardening journalist for the Telegraph, and copious blogger has managed to create one of the most acclaimed gardens in the country.

The four-acre garden, Veddw House, lies outside the village of Devaudan in Monmouthshire. Yorkshire-born Wareham, who originally trained as a social worker and psychotherapist, moved here from London in 1987.

She found the house by drawing a circle on a map on the borders of England and Wales, a part of the country she hardly knew at all, and where at first she felt lonely and out of place. 'I still don't know why in the hell I do the gardening,' says Wareham. She claims no sunlit memories of childhood gardening. 'All I remember was being paid a ha'penny to collect a bucket of dandelions', she says. But her life and new career has been shaped by an absolute conviction that she wanted a garden, and it was not going to be ordinary.

Veddw House is an incredible achievement. The garden, which she created with her husband, the gardening photographer Charles Hawes, has twenty-five distinct areas including a magnolia walk, a hosta walk, and a woodland walk. At its centre is a dark reflecting pool of stunning simplicity.

This is the place where Wareham can be found on summer evenings, with a glass of wine before supper looking at the way the light hits the bank of trees behind it, how it reflects the constantly changing skies of Monmouthshire. These fleeting moments of delight are the point and the pleasure of her garden.

To create this without becoming the garden's unwilling martyr and slave requires wit and cunning and an animal determination to stay one step ahead of nature.

I SPEND TWO TO
THREE HOURS IN BED
EVERY MORNING –
THE WORLD CAN'T
GET AT YOU IN BED

My day

'My motto in life is "do the big things first" so I spend two to three hours in bed every morning. The world can't get at you in bed. After an apple, and copious amounts of coffee, I write, answer e-mails, run my website and think about garden administration.

I get up around twelve, and for the rest of the morning do the housework and all the other stuff you avoid by being in bed. I don't have children, or a dog.

Afternoons, I go to the office and that's when the serious work begins: either on a book or a blog, about the garden or about human relationships, or a Telegraph piece.

I've always written quickly and concisely and can write an essay in a couple of hours. At some point in the day, I'll walk around the garden and look at it. If there is something to do, Charles and I work on it, but not every day.

It was lonely here at first. The Tintern Philosophy Group (run by Professor John Clarke) which meets monthly at the Rose and Crown, saved our sanity, and of course, the garden, which gave me a new life. One of the paradoxes is that, although I enjoy the fact that if I put up a question on twitter I might get two dozen responses, I'm essentially a private person. I would not like to open the garden to the public every day. It's only open on Sunday afternoons, and we don't do teas!'

Sally
Bailey

BAILEYS HOME

Sometimes you take a big leap and hope that the net is there, thinks designer and businesswoman Sally Bailey. In 2012, the eponymous Baileys, which she founded and runs with her husband Mark, won the Telegraph's Best Homeware Retailer of the Year, accolades from business super nanny, Mary Portas, who described it as one of her favourite stores, and a turnover in excess of a million pounds.

But in 2003 it was terrifying. That was the year that Sally and her husband Mark gambled on expanding the business by buying a rundown farm in the rural hinterland between Ross-on-Wye and Hereford. She recalls, 'We gave ourselves a major scare with two years of renovations that went way over budget.'

Today the business, which sells an eclectic mixture of vintage and new household goods, is constantly evolving. Their aim, says Sally, is to sell 'simple, useful, well-made things', with their mantra being to rescue, re-cycle, and re-use, whether it's some beautiful old floor-boards being ripped up from a cottage in the mountains, or simple wooden toys designed by a Black Forest wood turner, or a consignment of beautiful bowls from a Paris flea market.

THE AIM IS TO SELL SIMPLE,
USEFUL, WELL-MADE THINGS
– RESCUE, RE-CYCLE, RE-USE

There are also ancillary businesses. They design and build pop up stores – a short term shop in someone else's store – for companies such as Liberty of London and Donna Karan in New York. They make a successful range of sofas, lights, and baths which are sold online and at the store. The business, which began as a family affair run by Sally, Mark, daughter Lucy 27, and son Ben 30, has grown to include twelve full-time staff. Their premises cover 930 square metres, the size of a small department store.

Sally, who exudes the kind of understated elegance most usually associated with French women, thrives on this life. Having left school at seventeen, she did a three year Diploma Course in design at Cardiff Art College before her first job with landscape designer Sheppard Fidler.

She met Mark in 1980. They were bidding against each other at an auction in Pontypridd. He was an antique dealer, who'd trained as a furniture designer. They started buying and selling as Baileys in 1983, originally working from the coach house and stables of their home. Today, the family live in the beautifully converted farmhouse, a stone's throw from the store. When they're not travelling, designing or buying, weekends are spent at a cottage in Clyro, near Hay-on-Wye.

My day

'If it's a work day, I'll get up early, jump into the shower, let our five chickens out, have breakfast, and get into work by eight. I go through the emails, and plan the day, the week, the month, and it's always different.

Last weekend for instance, I drove to Carmarthen to an antique fair, or we might go to Paris for trade shows, flea markets, or antique fairs. Often people come to show us what they have. For instance, a couple who live in France have just called in with the most beautiful stoneware jars and blue work wear jackets. Needless to say we bought everything.

I love being busy, I love the buzz of working here – the fact that no two days are ever quite the same. There are always crises, something to solve, but we've learned to chill as we get older. Mark and I work well together, probably because there is a clear division of tasks – Mark does the displays and the antique buying, I do the buying for the stores. Occasionally, we have a set to and then the staff hide under their desks, but mostly it works, and we do have a rule at home: no ranting after nine o'clock at night!

It's all about the quality of your life, not constant work. Last week we drove to Builth Wells to hear a Russian pianist, we go to the theatre occasionally, or to see the Welsh National Opera. We relish the variety of life here, the fact that we live surrounded by glorious countryside, and there's always someone interesting walking through our door.'

Angharad Davies

BARRISTER

Angharad Davies, 36, has always looked young for her age. Catch her off duty, in shirt and jeans, you might mistake her for a small pretty teenager walking an awfully large dog. Catch her in court, in wig, her black gown, in two inch suede high heels, listen to her speak with precision and self confidence, and you'll see the highly professional, very confident barrister she is. She enjoys the transformation and is keen to see traditional court dress preserved. The putting on of the gown is the putting on of power in a profession she's fought hard for.

The law is still overwhelmingly dominated by men. 50% of law students are women, only 35% of them are called to the Bar, and few make it to the top. Angharad admits that without hard work, luck, timing and bloody-mindedness she would never have made it.

Born on the Sussex/Surrey border, to a father who was ex-R.A.F, and a mother who rode racehorses at a Newbury stable, she and her brother were educated at The Weald Comprehensive School. From as far back as she can remember she wanted to be a barrister, but her school had no big dreams for her. Her careers adviser suggested an office role for her. 'Yes, depressing isn't it ?' That or somebody's assistant.' She ignored their advice.

At fifteen, resourcefulness changed her life. She was singing in a church choir with a successful barrister who had become a judge, Registrar Malcolm Buckley, who worked in the Royal Courts of Justice in London. She asked if he could help her get work experience.

THE SCHOOL'S CAREERS ADVISER THOUGHT I MIGHT BE GOOD IN AN OFFICE ROLE

MY SPECIALITY IS LAND AND DEAD PEOPLE

Shortly after that she was sitting in the Old Bailey just behind Counsel defending a woman accused of a gruesome murder. 'I was right there in the body of the court.' Her eyes still shine at the memory, 'enthralled, hooked by how they were trying to help someone who had such a poor case. The only thing that upset me was when I wasn't allowed to see the crime scene pictures. They said I was too young'.

She got six A-levels, a law degree at Swansea and spent a year at the Inns of Court School of Law in Gray's Inn, London. 'Terrifying and stimulating in equal measure,' she recalls. 'You're plunged into a highly charged competitive world of hugely clever people with swathes of arrogance, and you're in small lecture groups so there is nowhere to hide. At first, I often went home in tears as it was so intimidating.' She quickly learnt to stand her ground.

Only one in six law graduates make it to the next hotly contested stage – the winning of a pupillage, an apprenticeship with an established barrister. After writing countless letters and attending interviews, she was accepted to do pupillage at New Square Chambers, Lincoln's Inn. In October 2000 she was called to the Bar by Lincoln's Inn. On the night of her call, her proud parents and Malcolm Buckley, the judge who had first helped her, saw her for the first time in wig and gown.

In 2000, Angharad moved back to Wales, where she now practices at Thirty Park Place Chambers, Cardiff. She appears in court on average twice a week, where her speciality is, she deadpans, 'land and dead people'.

The job is challenging and the hours can be extremely long, making it important to have a balanced domestic life. It helps that her partner Hefin is a lawyer. 'But I love the work,' she says. 'It's different everyday; it's intellectually challenging, and I wouldn't do anything else.'

Home is a nineteenth-century stone cottage in the Wye Valley. They are slowly renovating the cottage, with the assistance of their Italian Spinoni dog, Bella.

My day

'I wake when the dog wakes, so usually when the sun rises. If I'm in court that day, I'll drop her off at her Doggie Day Care (her kennels) en route to Cardiff, where she happily spends the day with other dogs. If I have a shorter paperwork day she guards the house until I return.

I am self-employed but work from a Chambers alongside a number of other barristers. We own and occupy the two Victorian buildings we work in, pooling resources and clerks.

Most mornings, I sit with my cup of tea at my old-fashioned leather-topped desk amidst piles of papers, deeds, wills and photographs and read and research cases. If I'm meeting new clients I will often meet them for a conference in Chambers or have a site visit.

It's often 3pm before I notice I haven't had lunch. On court days, it's a fifteen minute walk to Cardiff Civil Justice Centre and I enjoy the walk. There I go into the robing room, get dressed in wig and gown and usually feel a pleasant adrenalin rush.

IT'S GOOD TO KNOW THAT YOU CAN FIND PEACE IN THE COUNTRYSIDE

It's common to meet your clients just outside the court for the first time. For them, going to court can be extremely stressful and emotional and I try very hard to make complicated things as simple and understandable as possible. It's also important to reassure them of your complete discretion because you need them to be open with you in order that you can give the best advice.

The job is high stress; it can involve very long hours and reading large amounts of documentation. I have a good memory for facts and recall of documents which is helpful.

If a big case comes in late in the afternoon or on a Friday, that's the end of your plans, so it's important to find good ways of letting off steam. I walk the dog every day, do regular Pilates and Yoga sessions and love to be outside in my garden. Although I spend much of my day reading I do love a good crime novel to help me unwind.

The best relaxation of all is spending time with my Welsh partner and walking the dog. What I particularly like about living on the Borders is that it is a wonderful mix of Welsh and English: the people I meet locally are very warm and communicative, they like a chat and a cup of tea, but they don't intrude into your life when you need the space to work.

I love the woods around our cottage, how they smell when it has rained and the sound of water from the streams that flow through them. The hills of the Wye Valley certainly keep you fit and there is a beautiful variety of landscape and places where you can find solitude when you need it.

Sometimes when you feel you've faced everyone else's woes during the day, it's good to know that you can find peace in the countryside.'

Nell Gifford

CIRCUS OWNER

It's springtime, and the organised insanity that is Gifford's Circus is about to hit town. All their performing staff: the Ethiopian jugglers, the skewbald horse, the pigeons, chickens, fabulous clowns, the Polish acrobats, the dancers, and the fourteen-piece band are in rehearsal tucked away on the farm in Gloucestershire where they live and rehearse.

I KNEW IT WOULD WORK, AND THE SKY IS STILL THE LIMIT.

If you haven't seen Gifford's Circus, you must. It's a circus in the really basic and old fashioned sense, in that you go with your kids to a village green and it's there, but it's also fantastic fun and inventive. It was founded in 2002 by Nell Gifford, a statuesque blonde, who still does some of the riding stunts as ring-mistress on horseback.

When Nell was eighteen years old, and about to go up to Oxford to study English literature, her mother had a serious riding accident which left her in a coma. Relatives decided Nell should be sent away to the United States, for a gap year summer. There, she worked for the innovative Circus Flora, putting up tents, selling tickets, riding a horse in the parade. She caught the circus bug in a big way, and when she got home decided to start her own. As you do!

The result has been a show which for many fans has become addictive. It's playful, surreal and, at the same time, serious in its intentions. When asked if she was amazed by its success Nell said: 'Not at all, I knew it would work, and the sky is still the limit.'

In 2010, Nell won the £10,000 Groucho Maverick Award which celebrates the individual who has 'broken the mould in the arts within the last year'. And it's a measure of its ambition that this year their director is Cal McCrystal, whose last show was directing, One Man Two Guvnors at the National Theatre.

Audiences have grown and the circus which made its reputation on village greens up and down the Wye Valley, and at the Hay Festival, has extended this year's tours further East, towards Newbury and London. Celebrity fans include Chris Evans, Tilda Swinton and Vivienne Westwood.

For the seven months of the year that Giffords is not on tour, home is Folly Farm, fifteen acres of Gloucestershire loveliness, with a mellow brick farm house at its centre, and a garden designed by Toti, Nell's husband, who is a well known landscape designer and inventive builder, as well as co-producer of this year's show with Nell.

On the day we arrive, the blossom is out, the lambs are being born, and the distinctive maroon Gifford's Circus caravans have sprung up in the fields around the house, plus the big top in the farmyard for daily rehearsals. Inside the large prop room Toti built, there's the catering truck serving the cast, two set designers sawing and painting, an actor sitting alone, brow furrowed learning his lines, children playing. Horses peer out of magnificent stables lined with stage scenery, two Brazilian acrobats sashay across the yard. The place feels eccentric and skew-whiff, also purposeful, professional, exciting. It makes you long to join the circus.

Nell Gifford sits at the centre of this whirlwind. She is beautiful, with tired rings under her eyes, a deep husky voice, and an understandably distracted air. No crime when you have a total staff of seventy, plus three-year-old twins Red and Cecil, and a circus about to hit town.

When we arrive, she's negotiating with a howling Red who wants her and her only. Nell delays the interview to console and laugh with the child. That done, we go down a long red painted corridor, papered with ecstatic letters from circus fans, and into her office where shelves are piled high with costume fabrics and she sits under a huge crystal chandelier, surrounded by bookshelves full of art, photography and design.

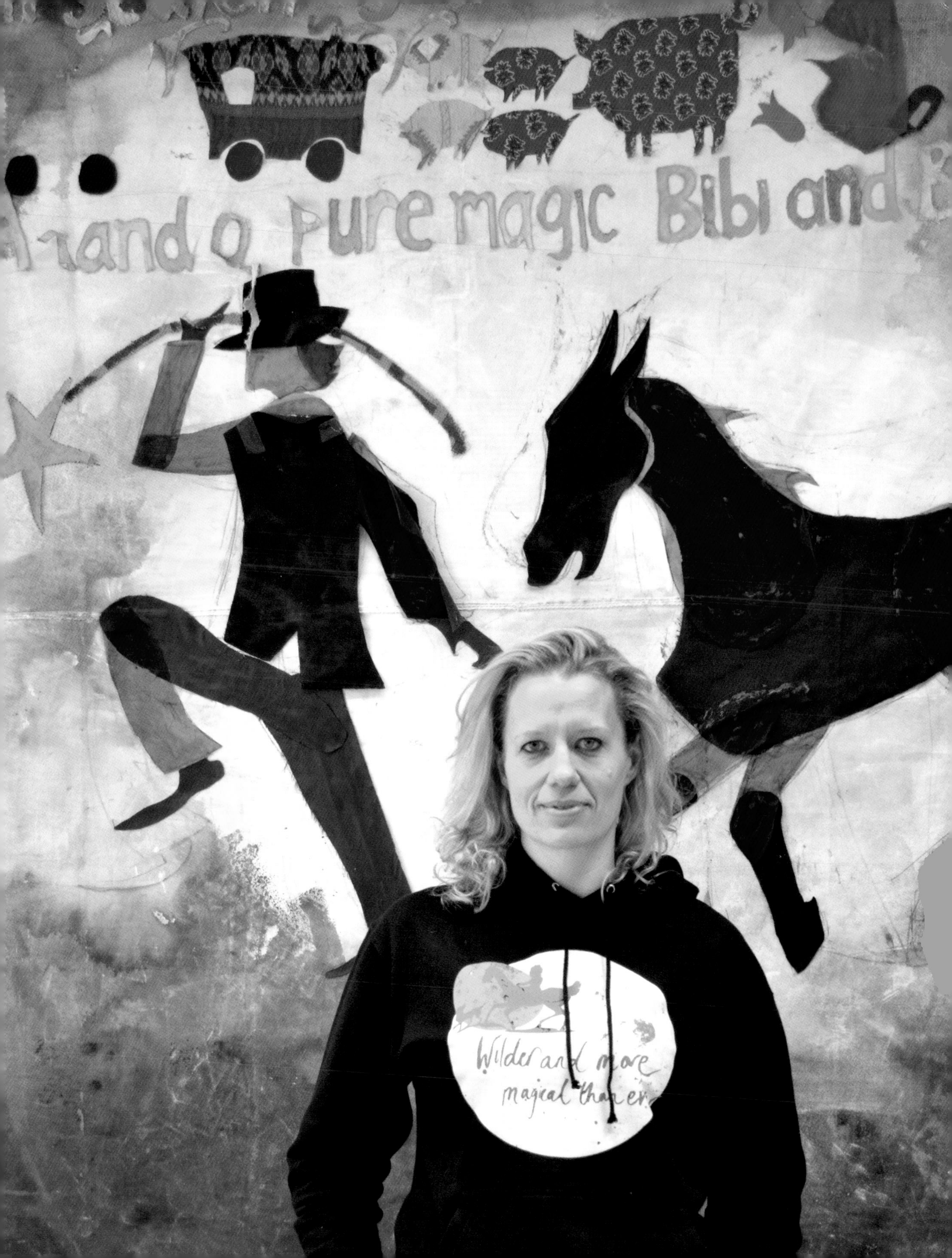
and a pure magic Bibi and
Wilder and more
magical than ever

My day

'I get up at seven in the morning, and do a series of exercises for one hour. Nothing fancy, but I like to keep fit because the pace is full on here and I'm still riding horses in the show.

While I'm working out, I keep an ear open for the mood of the day – how is everyone feeling? Who's up, who's down? My nanny, Daniella, gets the twins up and then I take them to school, a lovely school half an hour away from here.

We rehearse the current show on a day by day basis, depending on what needs most work, so I spend a lot of time with Cal, our director, and drop into as many rehearsals as I can. Much of what we do is improvisational, but it's also quite disciplined and structured too.

Next, I'll ride the horses and speak to the yard manager and their trainer. One of the downsides of circus life is ill informed bitching from people who assume circus animals have a miserable existence. It's not true: our horses are well loved and they enjoy their work and have lots of time off when they're not performing to just veg out in the fields and be horses.

Lunch is a rushed affair, often at the canteen, then it's admin: checking bookings, looking at proofs of programmes, organising sites, publicity, budgets. Sometimes we'll run improvised workshops in local villages, where we'll teach people how to have fun on stage, and the way an actor prepares.

The circus life is hard work, it's like spinning plates, but what makes it addictive is that it is really, really good fun the way we do it.

My husband Toti is an incredible man: he can build or do anything. I've just asked him to make us a grand piano for one set, and he'll do it. He built this barn – that fireplace looks as if it's been there for hundreds of years.

I like working hard, I like being creative, I'm so satisfied in what we do and what we've achieved, but we haven't reached our limit yet. That said, you have to learn when to stop, and over the years, I've got better at pacing myself. Afternoons are when I pick the children up from school, and then we'll almost always go for a ride together and have some quiet time. Both Red and Cecil enjoy the circus, but we never make them perform, if they're in the mood they might dash into the ring at the end.

I'll usually have dinner with Toti and then who knows? We're never bored or lonely, people drop in all the time. Cal brought down tons of interesting and strange films for us to watch and be inspired by, so we might watch one of them. During the season, it's pretty much non-stop socialising all the time. If we get to bed by 10pm it feels like a massive achievement.'

Caroline Peters

CHIEF SUPERINTENDENT, HEAD OF OPERATIONS AVON & SOMERSET CONSTABULARY

Picture this: you and your family are asleep at home in Penallt, a peaceful hilltop village overlooking the Wye Valley. The phone rings at 3am letting you know that the following has happened.

(a) There has been a major traffic accident on the M5, with some fatalities.

(b) A potential terrorist attack at the Hinkley Point power station with hostages held there.

(c) A murder has taken place in Bristol.

THE PACE IS PUNISHING BUT I DO LOVE THIS ROLE

If you are Chief Superintendent Caroline Peters, Head of Operations for the Somerset and Avon Police, you must decide how to deal with each scenario. Will you need to call in the bomb squad? An armed response? A helicopter? A homicide team? What horses? Dogs? Firearms?

Whatever hour of the day or night you get the call, you get up, put on your police uniform, creep out of the house so as not to wake husband and three kids, and hare off for another adrenalin packed day at the Portishead Headquarters of the Somerset and Avon Police. You will have a staff of three hundred and sixty working under you, an annual budget of approximately twenty million pounds, and, if you are Caroline Peters, think yourself the luckiest woman on earth to have this enormous and demanding job.

In person, Peters defies every stereotype served up in television series such as The Killing, Spiral, or Broadchurch, where female police officers are portrayed as grimly driven obsessives, so fixated by work that they sleep in their cars, shout at their colleagues, and privately weep for their marriages and children their ambition has ruined.

Peters, 45, is a good looking strawberry blonde with an unhurried air, and a luminous smile. Her manner is open, confiding, friendly. She has three children Holly 14, a scholarship pupil at the Royal Ballet School, Amy 12, and Paige 4. Her face lights up when she mentions her husband Mark, himself an ex-policeman. 'My family life is at the core of everything I do,' she says. 'But without Mark's support and love, it couldn't work. He is remarkable.'

Born and brought up in Luton, Peters was by her own admission, an underachiever at school, more interested in sport – she played tennis for the county – than lessons. Her Damascene moment came at age of fourteen when she was at the infamous football match between Luton and Millwall, where fans ran amok. 'It was frightening, a lovely day gone wrong: my seat was ripped from under me. And then I saw the police come in with their dogs. They caught the hooligans and restored order. It may sound naff but I was hooked.'

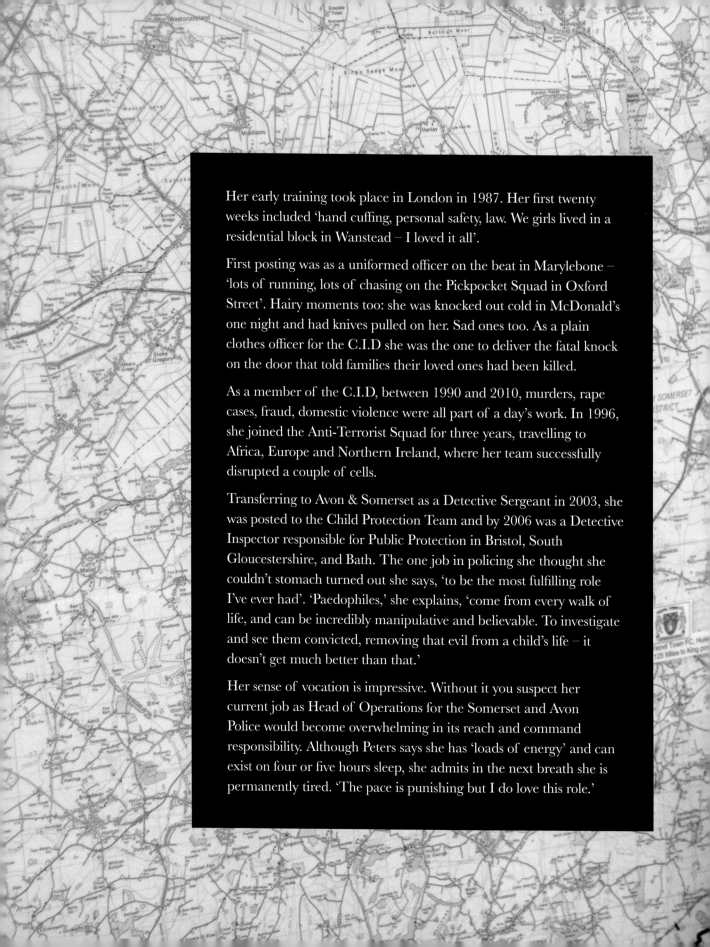

Her early training took place in London in 1987. Her first twenty weeks included 'hand cuffing, personal safety, law. We girls lived in a residential block in Wanstead – I loved it all'.

First posting was as a uniformed officer on the beat in Marylebone – 'lots of running, lots of chasing on the Pickpocket Squad in Oxford Street'. Hairy moments too: she was knocked out cold in McDonald's one night and had knives pulled on her. Sad ones too. As a plain clothes officer for the C.I.D she was the one to deliver the fatal knock on the door that told families their loved ones had been killed.

As a member of the C.I.D, between 1990 and 2010, murders, rape cases, fraud, domestic violence were all part of a day's work. In 1996, she joined the Anti-Terrorist Squad for three years, travelling to Africa, Europe and Northern Ireland, where her team successfully disrupted a couple of cells.

Transferring to Avon & Somerset as a Detective Sergeant in 2003, she was posted to the Child Protection Team and by 2006 was a Detective Inspector responsible for Public Protection in Bristol, South Gloucestershire, and Bath. The one job in policing she thought she couldn't stomach turned out she says, 'to be the most fulfilling role I've ever had'. 'Paedophiles,' she explains, 'come from every walk of life, and can be incredibly manipulative and believable. To investigate and see them convicted, removing that evil from a child's life – it doesn't get much better than that.'

Her sense of vocation is impressive. Without it you suspect her current job as Head of Operations for the Somerset and Avon Police would become overwhelming in its reach and command responsibility. Although Peters says she has 'loads of energy' and can exist on four or five hours sleep, she admits in the next breath she is permanently tired. 'The pace is punishing but I do love this role.'

My day

'If I'm on call, the day might begin at home at three in the morning with a call from H.Q, in Portishead, or if there's a major incident, I might be sleeping there. Back at home, Mark will be getting the children up for school, packing their lunches, walking the dogs.

At the office, my first job of the day is to read the overnight brief. Last night for instance it was the kidnapping of a schoolgirl, later found; a school caught on fire; there was a fatal road accident.

My job is to ensure the right specialist resources are in the right place at the right time. Sometimes there is a spontaneous event that requires decisions to be made very quickly, whether it is the threat of public disorder or a firearms threat. I am a Strategic Firearms Commander and with that comes a greater responsibility, to ensure the public are safe at all times.

MY FAMILY IS MY SANITY, AND SO IS LIVING IN THE WYE VALLEY

Next, I'll sit down with members of the team, and plan the biggest priority of the day: coming up we have policing for the G8 summit and the Glastonbury Festival.

Glastonbury is the biggest festival in Europe – 177,000 people converge on a working farm in Somerset over five days. Our main objective is public safety and preventing crime, so we'll have horses, dogs, police officers, working with the festival staff.

It's usually a ten to twelve hour day. At meetings with my fellow workers, I encourage brevity. I eat at my desk, I know it's a bad habit, but no time.

To relax, when I get home I spend quality time with Mark, Amy and Paige. Holly's off at the Royal Ballet School now. The kids are often asleep when I get home.

'It hasn't all been plain sailing. Our daughter Amy is autistic. She didn't speak until she was five, and had significant behavioural problems. We went through every emotion in the early years, and had to constantly fight for support. Now thanks to the family and great local support, she's a joy of a child – she speaks, she swims like a fish, in fact, having recently been selected for the Disability Wales Fast Track Scheme, she has started training with the Paralympic Swimming team, she's a pocket rocket. Amy is a very special young lady who enriches our lives – we're all better people for it.

Another major shift in our gears came recently when we took the decision to adopt three-year-old Paige. Following my years in Child Protection I had always harboured a desire to give a child a safe and loving home, but it had to be the right decision and more importantly a family decision. I don't like to dwell too much on the fact that she is adopted now, she's very much part of the family and is loved very much. Having just started school, she is progressing very well.

My family is my sanity, and so is living in the Wye Valley. Weekends are when my husband insists in a very sweet way that we have family time, and I totally agree. We walk as much as we can with the dogs, I play tennis, we have family meals together, we have treasured holidays away.

Although the job is always in my head, as I go home over the Severn Bridge, my phone looses its signal, the countryside gets prettier and prettier, and I can feel myself switching off, and being calmed by this incredible place.'

Jean
Miller

PAINTER

Jean Miller's door was flung open on Lion Street when we arrived at her house in Hay. The long, narrow corridor leading to her sitting room crammed with her own bold, brilliantly coloured, confident paintings. 'Matisse on speed,' is how art lecturer and painter, Cecily Sash describes them in her introduction to a recent book called Jean Miller's Paintings.

What is startling is that Miller, 83, who now has buyers from all over the world, and who had a sell-out exhibition at the Hay Festival last year, only started painting at the age of 68.

In person, she is feisty, opinionated, great company, in spite of the cancer that occasionally lays her low. Asleep on a green chaise longue when we arrived, she's not at all embarrassed when she wakes up to find us looking down at her. She says she's learned to accept herself as she is: ill at times, but still full of life and sustained by an urgent need to paint.

Miller's life was always unconventional. Educated at a boy's prep school in Folkestone where her grandfather was headmaster, she learned French at five, and Latin at six, as well as boxing, football, gymn and dancing. Next came the girls' school in Windsor where she was top of the form in her first term, and bottom by the end of the year. 'I was bored: I'd done all the work before.'

AFTER MY HUSBAND DIED, I THOUGHT, WHAT IN THE HELL ARE OLD WOMEN SUPPOSED TO DO?

A talented dancer, she later won a scholarship to the Bellair School of Dancing (the now famous Guildford School of Dance and Drama). They were taught there by a ballet teacher who'd been with the Russian ballet. It was the middle of the war. They were always hungry. They danced all day and did one hour of lessons, taught by a gardener turned maths and English teacher, which suited her down to the ground. At 17, she got a job, singing, dancing and acting, in the 'naughtiest show in town', Sweetest and Lowest with Hermione Gingold.

At Windsor Rep, in the early fifties, she met her future husband, Michael Miller, who proposed to her two days after they met. He was Henry the Eighth to her Anne Boleyn in 1066 and All That. The play was a smash hit. The Queen and Prince Philip saw it. They were married six weeks later, and for years after that were busy theatricals. Jean later went on tour with Dame Flora Robson. In her book Jean says: 'Flora was a marvellous actress, but I didn't get on with her. She always said you could tell someone with good diction because they'd spit, and whenever I was acting close to her, she was always busy spitting in my face.'

The constant separations of married theatrical life drove the Millers to move to Jersey, where they rented a Georgian house for £4 a week, had three children, and ran a market garden which eventually went bust. Michael went back to acting until a terrible car accident put an end to a successful career that included films with Richard Burton and Peter O'Toole.

'For 21 years after the accident, he was messed up,' Jean recalls. 'Life was difficult but we got through it.' To make ends meet, and with no formal training, she cooked pies for posh shops in London, such as Justin de Blank, discovering that if you put 'pheasants and grouse into pastry you could charge six times more than if you put beef and bacon in'.

Widowed at 68, and exhausted by the cooking, she moved to Hay-on-Wye where the greatest adventure of her life began. She discovered she was a painter.

My day

'After my husband died, I thought, "What in the hell are old women supposed to do?"

I'd moved to Hay, bought a house, put a green carpet down, then the furniture. I'd tried volunteering at the Red Cross, now what? My daughter Polly said, "You could draw once, have a go at that." So I did.

I went to the community centre once a week for a two-hour art class and as soon as I started I thought: I can do this. It was in the genes: my grandfather went to the Slade where he met Monet; my sister was a scenic designer.

The next year, I went to Hereford Art College with all these young people – they'd be off for a cup of coffee, I was hard at it. I had an exhibition at Addyman Books while I was there. My tutors thought I was being conceited, but the exhibition was a success, and I've never looked back.

Painting has been my salvation. Eight years ago, when I was diagnosed with cancer, my oncologist said, "go home and paint", and that's what I've done.

MY ONCOLOGIST SAID, GO HOME AND PAINT, AND THAT'S WHAT I'VE DONE

In the morning, I'm a housewife and quite disciplined: I shop, cook, wash and tidy up.

After shopping, I come home and have a nap, then I paint in the afternoon in a studio I've fixed up at the top of my house.

I paint very fast, often listening to Radio 4 but not listening, because when it's going really well, you get completely lost. Usually, I start with red because it gets me going, and I try not to analyse too much.

I had an active childhood, and now I'm having an active old age. There's no Saturday, and no Sunday. I can't travel much now because of the cancer, and I don't do publicity, but the paintings keep selling and now I can't imagine my life without this. When the Hay Festival is on, I open my house to whoever wants to come and the world comes in.

In 2012 I sold 15 oils and 20 prints, and last year I had a marvellous festival but ended up in hospital with exhaustion, hey ho, what a to-do.

Last thing at night, I go up and look at what I'm painting, and first thing in the morning.

Will I ever stop? I hope not. Leonardo da Vinci said you know when to stop painting because an angel touches you on the shoulder. I don't have any angels, just this.'

Hannah Stone

ROYAL HARPIST

If people were colours, Hannah Stone would be gold.

She is golden in appearance: an old fashioned blonde bombshell, with an hour glass figure and a gorgeous face.

As Official Harpist to the Prince of Wales, she plays a £150,000 gold leaf harp made by the Italian harpist, Victor Salvi. The harp belongs to the prince, the talent is hers: at the tender age of 26, critics are already saying she is one of the best harpists in the world.

THE HARP BELONGS TO THE PRINCE, THE TALENT IS HERS

So far, so romantic, and there's more: two years ago, she married the handsome young baritone, Gary Griffiths, who won the coveted gold medal at the Guildhall School of music and who is now a rising star – the next Bryn Terfel they say – in the opera world.

But here the fairy tale must end, because Hannah is a down to earth professional, and a harp, golden or otherwise, may sound ethereal and other worldly, but you need physical strength to carry the thing – her own harp weighs roughly 80 lbs and is 6'1" high. It is also a notoriously difficult instrument to play, demanding many hours of practice to master its intricacies.

Stone, who grew up in a Welsh-speaking home in Swansea, and later the Mumbles, began her apprenticeship aged eight. Her Dad is a policeman who loves music, her mother a nurse who plays the piano, and brother Gareth is a talented pianist and violin player. Educated at Ysgol Gyfun Gwyr Comprehensive School in Swansea, there were no pushy stage parents or teachers; she was never nagged to practice. 'The spark was always there.'

Semi professional from the age of fifteen, she went on to study at the Guildhall School of Music in London, followed by two years postgraduate work at the Royal Welsh College of Music and Drama. Prizes and awards swiftly followed, galas with Dame Kiri Te Kanawa, concerts all over the worlds, master classes for children. Being organised is important too, so she must be practical, in order to catch planes and organize an increasingly hectic schedule. She's not complaining. We first met her at Dore Abbey, a Cistercian monastery in the Golden Valley where she was performing with her husband. A freezing rain-lashed night made magical by their youth and talent.

I PRACTICE THREE HOURS IN THE MORNING SEVEN DAYS A WEEK

On the wet and windy morning we met at the Welsh College of Music and Drama, she's been up early walking dogs, doing her three hours morning practice, packing the dresses for our photo session, making arrangements for a concert she was about to do at St. Asaph Cathedral in North Wales.

When the camera was ready, she's changed, in a flash, from damp street clothes into a sensational gold sequinned dress, closes her eyes briefly, then plays a Bach Lute Suite in C Minor, alone under the spotlight, on a large empty stage.

In conversation, she is reserved, a little shy – although wary might be more accurate. The job of Royal Harpist has brought her into the heart of the Royal household, of which she is now, officially, a member. Part of her remit is to play at lavishly choreographed State occasions, at charity dinners, at public and private concerts. When she plays for the Queen, or Charles, or Heads of State, she might sit only feet away from them. It's a fascinating, privileged ringside view of history, but careless talk would be fatal.

Next year, she'll be recording Lullabies of Harp Music for the Royal baby, George, with The Cardiff Acapella Group. There's a solo album in the offing; new pieces to learn fit for a King. The excitement, the stress, the sacrifice, she accepts with an outward calm: it's part of the art that art conceals, and in one so young, it's impressive.

My day

'I have two sorts of days: home days when there are no gigs, and work days, when I'm touring, or recording, or teaching. Both hectic!

You need stamina to lead the life I lead, so on a home day, I make a conscious effort to stay fit either by running, if there's time in half marathons, or playing squash. Either way, I'm out before breakfast to walk our two pugs around the Bay.

I practice three hours in the morning seven days a week. After that it's usually a long lunch and in the afternoons I'll do admin, more practice, or if one of my three teachers are around, I might have a lesson. I love being taught, being stretched, learning new pieces, and one of the few frustrations of my life is that I don't have enough time for this.

This is a very very hectic time in Gary's life too. He's just been offered the role of Figaro in New Zealand opera, and is often away touring. When he's back and working with the Welsh National Opera it's a treat to have him home.

Our life revolves around music. This year, when we went on holiday to a cottage in St. David's my harp came too. But we're not all about music – we love going out for a drink together, and I enjoy cooking for him.

I try not to play past about six at night, so we can relax and be together. We're one hour from Swansea here, and we go and see my family whenever we can.

I love living in Cardiff: it's very Welsh, but close to London too, and close to the most incredibly beautiful places like the Wye Valley, where you can walk, and breathe. The adrenalin rush of doing a concert can be great, but there are lows too – the times when you do a performance and you think, you've really nailed it, but you don't get the response, and sometimes, you're praised and you're not satisfied. So it's good to step back, talk to the dogs, or the trees to see your life in perspective.'

Venetia Williams

RACEHORSE TRAINER

You cross a bridge over the Wye. Drive down an avenue of russet and gold horse chestnut trees. An imposing Palladian style house appears and you might have stepped into the opening pages of a Jilly Cooper novel. It's not just the emerald green fields on either side of you filled with thoroughbred horses, including Mon Mome, her Grand National winner in 2009, or the Aston Martin in the drive. It's Venetia Williams herself; tall, immaculately dressed, charming – she was described as elegance personified by one swooning male sportswriter from the Racing Post.

Walk through the sunlit hall filled with framed photographs of winners, and into the tidy office at the side of the house. Here, Williams and her staff of thirty five oversee the training and fitness of eighty five horses – in today's economy, it's a thriving and successful operation.

Venetia, who describes her philosophy of life as, 'hope for the best and expect the worst', caught the racing bug young from grandparents who kept and trained racehorses. After school she was apprenticed with trainer John Edwards and was a talented and successful amateur rider (ten wins) before a near fateful fall when she was eighteen. She was ahead of the field on a 33-1 outsider in a race at Worcester. Her horse took off too far from the fence, her head was plunged into the earth at roughly thirty-five miles an hour.

'Earth, sky, earth, sky, the fall seemed endless, and then I felt grass on my face. The rest of my body suspended in a thousand pieces above my head, and then I couldn't feel anything.' It was a hangman's fracture, an inch either way and it could have killed her.

EVERYTHING WENT
MENTAL IN 2009
WHEN MON MOME
WON THE GRAND
NATIONAL AT 100-1

She spent the next two months in Worcester Hospital. 'I was in denial. I kept thinking, I'm definitely going to race ride again.'

Instead she became a trainer. At first, an anomaly in a man's world, and one with unconventional training methods. 'Many racehorses live artificial lives, cooped up in stables when they're not racing,' she says. 'But here we give them two hours of turnout every day so they can live like horses; get muddy, roll, see their friends. It's expensive to keep horses, and you get no brownie points for muddy, happy horses if they don't perform.'

But perform they did, her reputation growing bit by bit, until everything went mental in 2009 when her horse, Mon Mome, won the Grand National at 100-1, the longest odds ever in the race's history.

'It was surreal,' she recalls, 'I could hear the cheers, I could see the horses. As they came into the last ten jumps I remember hearing the commentator saying: "Any one of twelve horses could now win this race," and I thought damn, we'll probably come in seventh because the prize money only goes down to sixth, then Mon Mome just surged ahead. I went into a weird state of shock watching him.'

And no, she hadn't placed a bet. 'I never do, the excitement is so not connected with money. It's connected with achievement, with pride in the horse and jockey.' But she will admit that the Grand National prize – £500,000 to the winner – was the best pay day ever, priceless in joy, priceless in the prestige it brings.

There was a huge party at her place that night – trainers, owners, anyone they could rustle up from their local village of Hoarwithy. 'We knocked on doors, we wanted everyone to come, we emptied the off-licence of champagne, we were so excited none of us could sleep. The joint was jumping until the following morning.'

Such hoolies are sweet but rare. What characterises life at the Williams' yard is a relaxed but highly disciplined approach, with up to a hundred horses in training, this year contesting around four hundred races. When asked if she's a nervous wreck being responsible for so much valuable horse flesh she answered no. 'My heart may pound at the start of a race, but I have learned to keep my emotions in check.'

When not at home, or flying to the continent to buy horses for owners, which she does frequently, Williams typically works a twelve to fifteen hour day.

YOU MUST SIZE UP THE OPPOSITION, THE WEATHER, THE GROUND, I'LL TALK TO MY STAFF, I WILL LISTEN, BUT I AM THE ONE WHO MUST MAKE THE FINAL DECISION

My day

'I wake around 7.15am, go into the yard and I feel all the horses legs. No breakfast, no time, we get the first lot of horses out on the all-weather gallops around 8am, and during the day four lots of horses go out at different times.

I used to ride out with them all the time, but now I ride out about once a week. What I'm doing mostly is watching them: how fit they look, how they're moving.

After that, it's back in the office. If you want to enter a horse for a race, you declare your runners between 9.15 and 10am. This is the game of chess time: Is this the right race for this horse? What are the weather conditions? How fit is the horse? You must size up the opposition, the weather, the ground. I'll talk to my staff, I will listen, but I am the one who must make the final decision.

In the afternoon, I'll talk to owners, or go to the races, or visit horses on box rest. There are inevitable injuries in training, it's like in athletics with humans, if you want to win races you can't train for them, you must take a horse to a place where he can perform.

It's rare to discover an equine Usain Bolt. In the early days Mon Mome was a very ordinary little horse, I bought him cheaply in France where he'd had one race – who knew he was going to surprise us like that?

I usually work until around 10pm at night because there are no distractions then. I travel miles every year. Living on my own means I'm incredibly grateful to local friends who ask me to dinner parties knowing my chances of reciprocation are nil. What I do is ask friends out for a day at the races, or we'll go on holiday somewhere.

I love living near the river. I like the people around here.

I'm lucky to lead the life I live.'

Andrea McLean

MAPPING ARTIST

MY MAP PAINTINGS ENCOMPASS MY LIFE EXPERIENCE – SHIFTING PATTERNS IN LIFE'S JOURNEY

When Andrea McLean was seven years old, her father lifted her up and showed her the Mappa Mundi in Hereford Cathedral. It changed her world.

'I knew from an early age that I wanted to paint, and drew constantly – huge black and white doodles on paper – but this was it: my talisman, and I found I wanted to create my own Mappa Mundi, and that everything I had thought, and dreamed and known should appear in my paintings.'

Her formal training began at Falmouth College of Art, and later at the Slade, where she won a year-long scholarship to study art in Rome. Rome was a revelation: 'I discovered frescoes, and artists like Lorenzetti, a way of painting that was both detailed and calm. I became interested in Blake – his idea of an imaginary city; the way he made his own mythology and found a way of sharing his visions.' She also started a lifelong habit of writing journals, detailed, lushly illustrated, that burst with sketches and ideas, poems, blue prints for future work.

When the year in Rome ended, McLean came back to 'the tap root', Ledbury, and a small house on the edge of town crammed with books and paintings where she lives and paints today. Ledbury is a fine place to live, she says: good coffee shops, an art gallery, good friends. Her closest friend is Tessa Frith, song-writer and singer. But, best of all, Andrea is close to the countryside she loves.

McLean is a luminous, quietly impressive presence; someone who you sense, notices and feels everything.

Her detailed, circular map-paintings – she is currently working on one 8ft in diameter – have been exhibited at the Royal Academy in London, and become popular with both collectors and churches throughout the land. Having been artist in residence at both Hereford and Gloucester Cathedrals, she is currently making a community map, leading workshops for people with dementia as 'I'm interested in the therapeutic nature of painting'.

Last year Andrea finished a large painting based on Blake's Jerusalem and two other paintings with religious themes for Easter Exhibitions. In the widest sense of the word, her paintings, with their mandalas and mystical signs, have a spiritual dimension.

They are the way she both expresses and heals herself, for McLean talks openly about being bi-polar and how it has both informed and sometimes held up her work. 'I feel its effects at both ends of the pole, sometimes with experiences that feel almost visionary, celebratory. But if it's a bad depression, there are times when I can't read, or think properly. I don't hide it, it's part of who I am. In general, I'm lucky to have work that sustains me so well, and when I'm low I walk a lot and rely on the poetry of nature to carry me through.'

My day

'The early part of my day is for reflection, so when the light wakes me up, around 7.30, I go for a two-hour walk in the hills above my house. The hills are quite steep around here, but I like seeing the world from above, and I look at everything. I always take a sketch book with me, but mostly I use these walks for looking: a great deal of the early work of a painting is about looking, paying attention. I'll sometimes take a piece of writing with me to reflect on, or I might write in my journal. When I get back, I'm full of energy and ready to go.

I LIKE SEEING THE WORLD FROM ABOVE, AND I LOOK AT EVERYTHING

Monday is for bills and admin, but if it's a painting day, I can go for long stretches – it could be for three or four hours, and then I'll stop and look things up, or maybe eat, and start again. I've been to Mexico and to India searching for colour, and am interested in the way they do things there. In India I found there are pilgrim maps, which plot the course of life; they show cities as sacred places, the sun, the moon. They are wonderful reminders of the breadth of life, a reminder not to narrow your focus, to be where you are.

My commissions often take me in a different direction to the main trajectory of my work. I'm currently making a painting inspired by Elgar's music for what was his study in Hereford. I've done several months painting in Shoreditch, East London, but the Borders are my home.

I think a lot about shifting borders and a way of painting that respects boundaries but shows the borderland as the special, almost magical place it is. I'll go on until about 10.30 or 11 at night, and often, I'll write up my journal, working over each page until it's complete.'

A STEVEN SPIELBERG FILM

Revel Guest

The last two years have been a time of storming professional triumphs for Revel Guest. The 81-year-old writer and film director produced the film of War Horse with Steven Spielberg, and, as Chair of the Hay Festival, she's been a key part of its phenomenally successful expansion into Colombia, Spain and 13 other countries.

But when, in 2011, a beloved six-year-old grandson died of an aggressive brain tumour, 'It put all of our lives into perspective,' says Revel who counts grandchildren as one of life's 'joyful surprises', and family as the most important thing in her life. 'And yet work was vital to some kind of recovery.'

Revel – the name comes from an ancestor, a defrocked priest – lives in bohemian splendour in a house called Cabalva, near Hay-on-Wye with panoramic views of the Wye River. She shares their 600 acre farm and grounds with her husband, Rob Albert, an American international lawyer, and her two children, Corisande and Justin, both of whom started their careers as lawyers and film makers. Now Justin is the National Trust's Director for Wales. Corisande has taken over running the farm and writes novels.

Together the family runs Transatlantic Films which has, since its inception forty-five-years ago, produced over a hundred and fifty films for the international television market and as Co-Founder and Executive Producer of Covent Garden Pioneer, Revel has produced fifteen full length opera and ballet productions from Covent Garden for the BBC, Channel 4, and subsequent international distribution.

Revel with her family on steps of Cabalva – husband Rob, son Justin, daughter Corisande and her six grandchildren, Theo, Ibby, Tommy, Iona, Oscar and Charlotte.

IT DOESN'T MATTER IF YOU'RE
A FILM MAKER, A JOURNALIST,
A LAWYER, OR A MOTHER, YOU
HAVE TO BE BRAVE.

My day

'When I ran the farm for thirty years I also trained and bred event horses and was an early riser, but now I'm up later at 8 am. After breakfast I deal with emails that could be about anything: the feature film I'm preparing at the moment, The Moon is Down, by John Steinbeck, or next year's Hay Festival, or a new documentary, An American Hero: Tommy Hitchcock, a character from the Great Gatsby, or a farming problem. Or I might be out in the garden picking vegetables for lunch. I'm impossible to work for because I jump from subject to subject and I do consider work play, and play work, with no division between the two.

Most mornings, I drive to Hay to the Festival office, where Peter Florence and I will work on the Festival. As Chair, my main job is to keep it financially sound. I feel passionately about the Festival, and we've been able to change it from a small local literary festival on the Welsh Borders to international festivals of ideas and culture.

In Hay, over a twelve-day period at the end of May, 200,000 people come together from all over the world. This is my favourite time of the year because everything I love is at hand.

We usually have a houseful of friends: Hannah Rothschild, Sabrina Guiness, Joan Bakewell, Nick Broomfield, Simon Schama, Jim Naughtie, Rosie Boycott are all regulars. Bill Clinton, who came one year, famously dubbed us "the Woodstock of the mind". It is a time when I love sitting up late at night and getting up early for breakfast the following morning … talking and eating and having wonderful conversations.

We're a very close family, often working on some project together. Rob, who I've been married to for 50 years, does the legal work for the films, farm and the Festival. Corisande and Justin, although working full time with their own families, are much involved with the Festival.

We all live in the Golden Valley and often have meals together. If I see grandchildren running towards me over the hill, all work stops … they take over. I've lived here since early childhood.

My father, Oscar Guest, brought the family here during the Second World War, and many of the curtains and chair tapestries in Cabalva were made by my grandmother, so there is a great sense of family history and continuity.

Rob and I go up to London almost every week and we travel all over the world, he for his law practice, and I for the Festival, however, when I'm at Cabalva and have a moment, I head straight out to the garden. I believe that if you are lucky enough to have your own eggs, fresh vegetables and fruit, and lamb from your farm, what more could one want … and survival is confirmed.

I can't pick out a highlight from my life. When I worked as an investigative journalist for Panorama it was heady stuff, you felt as if you could effect some important changes.

Now that I'm older, I feel extraordinarily lucky that I am healthy and still working at things that I love. One of the reasons why I felt so pleased and excited to get War Horse off the ground was that it's a film about loyalty, about the disastrous consequences of war, and about bravery … which is key. It doesn't matter if you're a film maker, a journalist, a lawyer, or a mother, you have to be brave.'

Kate Beavan

FARMER & RURAL SKILLS TEACHER

Kate and Jim Beavan should come with a warning label thinks T.V. presenter, Kate Humble. Last year she went to a one-day course at Kate's Country School, near Abergavenny. This year Humble has her own farm with her own flock of sheep and has just gone through her first season of lambing with the Beavans on speed dial.

Three years ago, the Beavans were completely unknown country farmers. They lived in a secluded valley at Great Tre-rhew Farm underneath the Skirrid near Abergavenny. It has been in the family for three generations. They worked their socks off – they once delivered 2,000 lambs in seventeen days. Like all farmers they worried about money, and then, because someone wanted to see lambs being born on television, they were asked to appear on a BBC series called Lambing Live.

An incredible post bag followed, 'boxes and boxes of letters', remembers Kate. It wasn't just farming folk that wrote in, it was merchant bankers, social workers, teachers. They had struck a chord which, even today, Kate finds hard to define. Was it nostalgia for the land at a time when a growing number of people were moving to the country and wanted to keep a few sheep or chickens? The growing realisation that we had lost sight of the animals who feed us, or simply that people enjoyed even for a few flickering moments on television being country dwelling hunter gatherers? Or, could it be the simple pleasure of watching three generations of a working farming family gathered in the kitchen, and the feeling of warmth this generated.

THE BEAVANS ARE A CLOSE KNIT FAMILY, TWENTY FOR CHRISTMAS THIS YEAR

'Farmers don't make much money,' Kate continues, 'and we were looking for some extra income, so I had a eureka moment. I thought, Jim's the best farmer around, and a great communicator, and we had this lovely old 12th-century barn which had a new roof, so let's try a few courses and see what happens.' Kate herself is a qualified lecturer in Animal Management, with a Masters in Environmental Conservation.

Today, Kate's Country School runs monthly classes in shearing, butchery, dry-stone walling, cider making, and of course lambing, and it's been a huge success. The farm is also a haven for wildlife, including otters and their habitats.

Kate is without doubt a vital part of this success. On the miserably wet March day we meet, she roars down the side of a field on a buggy: no make-up, torn overalls, windswept hair, but so happy looking she makes you smile.

The yard is full of mud, they've been lambing continually since January. A difficult year with heavy snows, and lamb diseases such as Schmallenberg virus to contend with, but 'we've still delivered 1,400 lambs', she says. She takes us into the kitchen, makes us tea, makes us comfortable, makes us laugh.

Further response to Lambing Live was from The One Show, making films which she found great fun, especially hatching eggs with Russell Brand amongst others! You can see it on YouTube.

In the summer they go to County shows, where Kate's Country School stands are much in demand and include shearing demos, lambing simulator, and the famous 'Guess the Poo' competition! 'Next, I'm off to a farming event in Olympia, London, to talk about diversification in farming,' says Kate.

She admits she was rubbish at geography as a girl, and when she came to Abergavenny, aged twenty-one to work as a veterinary nurse, she actually thought it was in North Wales and closer to Lancashire where she grew up. In Abergavenny, she met Jim at Young Farmers. After renting a house down the road for fifteen years, they finally moved to the family farm in 2007. The Beavans are a close knit family, twenty for Christmas this year, their support is vital. Farming, she admits, is still a tough way to earn a living – she's been to two farmer suicide funerals in the last few years. 'But it's not all doom and gloom either, and if it's in your blood you can't imagine doing anything else.'

National
How to deliver a lamb

My day

'It was pitch black out when I woke up at four am this morning. I put my overalls over my nightie and went to the shed which is a few yards from our back door. There are about 200 ewes inside the shed waiting to give birth, and the first thing you do is to stand and listen: there's a sound ewes make when they're lambing, they 'talk' during contractions.

Between four and six am, I delivered three lots of twins and a single. I spray the umbilical cord with iodine to prevent infection, check the ewe has got colostrum and that the lamb is suckling, and leave them together in a bonding pen. You would think I'd be used to it by now, but standing in the shed and seeing them delivered safely and calmly is one of the best feelings in the world for me.

Around five am, I answered emails and finished an article for Farming Weekly. This is my quiet time, and also when I'll do the cooking, usually a stew or a soup done in the slow cooker.

I woke the children up next – Sam is fourteen now, and Celyn (Welsh for Holly) is twelve – they have breakfast and the school bus picks them up at the end of the drive.

Next, I took some coffee up to Jim who did the night shift until two am, then got cleaned up, grabbed some marked assignments and went off to Usk College where I teach Animal Management two days a week between midday and six pm.

Admin and meetings drive me crazy, but I love the teaching: it's varied and fascinating. One of my recent pupils went off to China to work with rescued bears, another works with big cats in Florida.

Back home, I'll check on the sheep again, and the cows and the pigs we raise, and then it's family time. We have supper together, and then for me, the bliss of a nice hot bath, a glass of wine, or if it's summer, I'll lie in my hammock over the brook near the sheep shed.

Kate's Country School runs once a month, and we get an incredible variety of people coming from all walks of life. The lambing courses are very hands on: pupils learn how to deliver lambs themselves, number the ewes, fix health problems. The drystone wallers build walls, but all courses seem to end up surprisingly with everybody in the Cider House!'

Ineke Berlyn

TEXTILE ARTIST & WRITER

Ineke Berlyn is an internationally acclaimed quilt maker and textile artist whose work has won prizes all over the world. Her connection with the River Wye is passionate and specific.

Two years ago she was in Rhyader, where the river begins, and where that most beautiful of all birds of prey, the red kite, have breeding and protection centres. 'The kites were on the verge of extinction,' she explains in her soft Dutch accent. 'But thanks to the locals their numbers are increasing. At two o'clock one afternoon I watched a farmer put meat out to feed them; the crows sitting and watching them, and then the kites swoop and pounce. It was a fabulous and unforgettable sight.'

Being Ineke, the moment was painted and recorded in one of a series of sketchbook journals she keeps. These journals, Sketchbooks and Journal Quilts and Journal Quilts, Dye & Print, Landscape in Contemporary Quilts, and her new book Collections are works of art in themselves, and have attracted an enthusiastic readership. The images she records: birds, weather, skies, trees, town and landscapes including the River Wye, serve as preliminary sketches for the exquisite colour quilts she creates.

Her red kite quilt took two years to make and it's easy to see why her work has become both collectable and a source of inspiration for pupils, who come from all over the world to learn from her innovative skills and ideas.

Born and educated in Holland, Ineke comes from a family who 'make things'. Her brother is a furniture maker, and it was an aunt who inspired her first by teaching three-year-old Ineke to knit.

I'M NEVER WITHOUT A SKETCHBOOK, THEY'RE THE VISUAL DIARIES OF MY CREATIVE JOURNEY

She came to England thirty five years ago when she met her English husband, John, in Utrecht on a rugby tour. The attraction was instant and mutual: 'We met at Easter and were married by September.'

Home is now a stylish airy barn, designed and converted by John, on the outskirts of Bromsgrove and in sight of the Malvern Hills. It's all white walls and carefully chosen pieces of glass, the walls acting as a backdrop to her stunning quilts. Lots of photographs too of their two children, Liske, a textile designer working for a fashion company, and Peter, who works in the car industry, and grandsons William and Reyer.

Both barn and studio are designed to be carbon neutral. 'We produce more energy than we use', and on the freezing cold day we visited it was cosy and inviting. Her vaulted studio, attached to the barn, buzzed with creativity, with students colour blocking, stitching, and comparing work. As a teacher, Ineke, who speaks four languages, and also teaches in France, Holland, and Ireland, describes herself as positive and constructive. 'I want people to have fun here and be inspired by the creative processes.'

While we talk John serves us tea and oat cookies. He was in retail until, he says, 'it went belly up', and jokes, 'I'm her slave now.' He designs her web pages, does all the cooking in the summer school, and never moans, she says, when she can't tear herself away from the studio. The impression you get is of a contented partnership, and of a strong family. During our interview daughter Liske wandered in, grandson William was cuddled on John's knee, supper was on the stove, and conversation easy and eager.

eyes that pierce looking for life

My day

'I'm usually up by eight, and I go for a half-hour swim. I keep fit to concentrate and keep my head straight. I have breakfast and am in the studio by nine, either to prepare for a course, or to do my own work. This is the time when John deals with emails, or helps with our on-line courses, or the books which we self publish.

Our years naturally divide between teaching and exhibiting here, and then periods in France, where we have a house at St Hilaire la Foret in the Vendée.

It's quiet there and it's where I do a lot of sketching and experimenting.

There's always something coming up: recently an exhibition in Scotland, in Loch Lomond. This year I'm exhibiting the dress collection at the Quilt Museum in York, and am also part of a touring exhibition with six friends, throughout the U.K. Further exhibitions are planned for next year in Netherlands and Germany.

I like making things. When my daughter got married I made her wedding dress, out of fabric I designed, and my own dress was inspired by her bouquet. I'm never without a sketchbook in my bag – they're the visual diaries of my own creative journey. Lunch comes and my husband has to peel me away from my work. I love what I do and find it hard to stop. I find much inspiration in the Welsh hills, and in the countryside around us. I have a sculpture of red kites in flight in my garden – and find their shape and line a constant influence. Then I'm back in my studio again, it draws me like a magnet.'

Elizabeth Haycox

QUEEN OF HAY?
I'M AN AMERICAN,
WE DON'T DO TITLES

If you want to make Elizabeth Haycox wince, call her The Queen of Hay. 'I'm an American', she says, almost brusquely, 'We don't do titles.'

O.K. In the last three years, she has bought the legendary Richard Booth's Bookshop, converted a warehouse into a cinema, and bought the eighty-acre golf club outside the town, now her home. She has also helped set up the trust that bought Hay Castle, formerly owned by the King of Hay, Richard Booth, but she is quick to point out that it is her husband, formerly a banker, now an entrepreneur, who supplies the readies, and the shared inspiration. She is 'the go fetch retriever'.

She's in jeans on the morning we meet, and an apron. Her extraordinary mane of red hair tied back. She's been waitressing in the new and very successful coffee shop at Richard Booth's Bookshop, and did the stocktaking the night before. When first asked for an interview she sounded wary, 'This is everything I dread – do I have to take my clothes off?' But in person, sitting in a sunlit window, she is funny, talkative and frank about the dramatic life changes – early widowhood, an earthquake, new love, firings, new countries – that brought her here.

Haycox, 55, was born in Oregon, and grew up North of San Francisco in Marin County. The eldest of five children, and the daughter of a writer father, she was, as a child, hungry for books. 'I'd lie on the top bunk with my flashlight on, imagining myself as a princess in a castle – using my pajamas for hair.'

I WAS THIRTY YEARS OLD, NEWLY MARRIED, AND THEN BOOM, IT CAME: 7.8 ON THE RICHTER SCALE

After a theatre major at college in Missouri, she worked briefly in summer stock (American rep), and later got a job in The Emporium, an upmarket San Francisco store, which she immediately loved and was good at. Within nine months she was, age nineteen, running the designer department at their flagship store, where, she remembers, 'I made all the mistakes of the young. I was too eager, too hasty. Most of the staff were over forty three, and union. They were not thrilled.

'So I learned about office politics: to listen, to learn, to never bitch or take sides.' Before that, the best brain training she ever received was as a cocktail waitress in the biggest singles bar in San Francisco. There, 'with a tray above my head, I had to memorise 12-14 drinks, and deal with drunks, with hysterics'. Not many of those in the Hay Café, but she won't forget your order.

She was in San Francisco in 1989, when the big earthquake struck. She was working unhappily and non-creatively, for a big manufacturer. 'It was like working for the army. I was 30 years old, newly married, and then boom, it came: 7.8 on the richter scale, a terrifying noise, time suspended, and all the bridges closed. I went home that night with the woman who was my boss and who I couldn't stand, and went to work the next day wearing her underwear. It was in every way, a life changing moment!'

She and her then husband, Ralph, an executive with a power plant company, moved to a country town in Oregon, where they lived in bucolic bliss, and adopted two sisters: Eliza, now 17, and Hannah 16. They later adopted Daisy, their half-sister. During this time they also fostered fifty children. 'That was nothing, as the eldest of five, I'd been diapering since I was a kid.' It was the best of times, and then her husband, aged forty three – 'fit, active, a bit of a dare devil' – went away on a boy's skiing trip one weekend, slammed into a rock and was killed. Her face freezes at the memory of it. 'The suddenness of it was terrible, the worst thing in life.'

'I'D LIE ON THE TOP BUNK WITH MY FLASH-
LIGHT ON, IMAGINING MYSELF AS A PRINCESS
IN A CASTLE – USING MY PAJAMAS FOR HAIR.'

She was forty three years old, a widow. For several years, work was her escape. The successful Bed and Breakfast business she ran from her house developed into a wedding planning company. On Monday, her night off, she treated herself to dinner at a local bar, and it was there one night, that two seats across from her, she saw a good looking man reading Colette in translation. 'I thought Oh Please!' She rolls her eyes at the pretentiousness. 'And there I was pretending to read the Wall St. Journal, something I never read. We chatted. Nice to speak to a man again. His name was Paul Greatbatch. He was an investment banker. He'd come to Hood River to do some wind surfing.'

She asked him to dinner at a friend's house, thinking it would be nice to have a man for a friend, they emailed afterwards for six months. She saved all the emails. In London where he lived, he took her to the opera. 'For the first time since Ralph died, I felt alive. London, where she eventually moved to be with him felt exciting and new and had nothing to do with me being a widow.'

She and Paul travelled together to Ludlow where there were once lots of Haycocks before they emigrated en masse to Oregon in 1853. They both loved books, and went annually to the Hay Festival – 'I'd never experienced anything like it, for ideas, for energy – we went to everything.' And it was mooching around the town afterwards that Paul, who was about to retire, saw a small sign in an estate agent's window, and said casually to her over lunch: 'D'you think we should buy Richard Booth's Bookshop?' The rest is an unfolding history, and with Haycox at the helm, an exciting unpredictable one.

My day

'I'm up around 6.30, to pack Daisy's school lunch, then into the garden to pick vegetables for the cafe. Work is three pronged. For six years, the bookshop was the overwhelming project. Richard Booth, its previous owner, had vision and loved books, but not buildings. When we moved in the shop we were told: there's a rat in the basement and it's almost dead. Plus the shop had no heat, a damp carpet, and a staff who made little offices out of shelves – they were all in hiding. The first thing was to tell the staff, who were very experienced, that no-one was going to get fired, everyone would get a raise, that I respected their wisdom, and hoped they would teach me. I wanted to be behind the scenes, with my books, making coffee.

I'd seen a picture of the Trinity Library in Dublin, green lights and long beautiful tables covered in books, comfortable places to sit. I thought: that's how I want it to look. For four years, I was here everyday supervising. At one point, we split the family, with me in Hay with the two youngest kids, and Paul in London. Our core business is the books and the café, then the cinema, a converted warehouse, grew out of it.

bureaucracy is my least favourite thing, but when you're spending public money, everything has to be accounted for, and it takes up a lot of time. Hay is a place full of ideas: some great, some rubbish, but already the castle is hosting educational and community events.

Lunch is a moveable feast, often in the cafe, or I'll skip it. Most days I'm in the bookshop: first in, last out. Daisy comes here after school to do her homework. We're home most nights by 6.30. Now that Paul is retired, we have dinner as a family, something easy and delicious. Paul is half Hungarian and incredibly smart, and full of ideas. He grew up on an estate in Chesterfield and went to Cambridge. He throws the stick, I go fetch.

The local people have gone out of their way to make us feel at home, and I love living here. I'm like Rebecca, or Miss Read – without gloves! I only go to London for appointments because I'm happiest here. On weekends I work, or I might walk in the Begwyns, or climb Hay Bluff, but let's face it, I work a lot.

We have eighty acres of land here, and live surrounded by cows and sheep, but in my bed at night, when the wind is blowing, I can hear the clock tower strike in Hay.'

In 2010, Hay Castle, a 1635 Jacobean mansion with a Norman keep came up for sale. It was two million pounds. We decided to gather interested people to buy it as a resource for the town. I'd rather write a cheque than ask for money, and

Jenny McLoughlin

AN ATHLETE WITH CEREBRAL PALSY LEARNS TO ROLL WITH THE PUNCHES

'I'll never forget the roar,' says Jenny McLoughlin. She heard it on the lap of honour around the Olympic Stadium. Eighty thousand people on their feet, cheering, crying, hollering at the sight of The British Paralympic Women's Relay team, crossing the line in the 4x100 metres final. They'd won a bronze medal. 'And it felt like gold,' says Jenny, 'because we so nearly didn't make it.'

'Before the race, I knelt down and had one thought in my brain: stay in the zone. Stay in the zone.' The zone being the place where you forgot the gut-twisting hugeness of actually being at the London Paralympics in your G.B. kit, after years and years of slogging around a training track in Cardiff. The wet mornings, the low moments when either injury, or Jenny's cerebral palsy, meant she felt rubbish.

It meant forgetting her parents sitting in a fever of excitement in the crowd. The money they'd spent, the long drives each week from Chepstow to Cardiff for training which her mum did after her own day job. Forgetting Darrell Maynard, her coach for six years, and his tough love methods. The Darrell who tries not to be sentimental. 'I'll train everyone who wants to run faster,' but who bit his fingernails while she was racing. 'I'll never top that memory,' she says. 'Running with the other girls, the flag flying above our heads, my parents there, my brother Simon there.'

It keeps her running now.

We meet at The National Indoor Athletics Centre in Cardiff, and to see Jenny in the distance: blonde, slight, pretty, running on her own around a vast track, is to see the slog side of that one shining hour.

It's almost a year after the Olympics. She's pulled an Achilles tendon, so training is restricted and she's missed a couple of crucial competitions already this year. The World Games, where she won Bronze two years ago in the 4x100m, and the Commonwealth Games where, in 2010, she won silver in the 100m.

No moaning from Jenny McLoughlin. An athlete with cerebral palsy learns to roll with the punches. Her CP – an umbrella term for a variety of symptoms – has left her with a pronounced weakness on the right side of her body, plus stiffness which would, she says, be much, much worse if she didn't run. She loves running for its own sake. 'I love the competition, the rigour of the training, though not always! The feeling afterwards of being spent.' And the good news is, as far as her CP is concerned, running is for her a great healer.

To meet her, wearing her GB track suit, and sipping water, is to forget she has any disability whatsoever: she is so vital, toned and fit looking. I doubt we'd have talked about it at all if I hadn't raised it. 'My parents have never made a big deal of it,' she says. 'There was no poor me, no talk of disability, they only said, "everyone has opportunities, take them".'

I'M 21, AND I FEEL AS IF I'M LIVING OUT EVERY OUNCE OF MY POTENTIAL

Born in Manchester, Jenny grew up in France where her father was a Programme Manager in aerospace industry, and where she and Simon went to school. When the family moved to Chepstow in 2005, she started to train with the Cwmbran Harriers, where she met Darrell, who saw in her a hard working perfectionist with the potential to go far. 'But we have to adopt an attitude of hope for the best and expect the worst,' he explains. 'You get tired with CP, and it's unpredictable. On a good day she can beat anyone, on a bad day she might come last. She doesn't complain. Half of all athletes jump ship because it is hard, but she was tough and determined.' There were, he admits a few panicky moments. 'I had to teach her to be self-sufficient, to manage her own blocks, her own kit, her nutrition, but now she has a set of skills that will be with her all her life.'

Two weeks after the Olympics ended, she started a philosophy degree course at Cardiff University. 'My aim now,' says Jenny, 'is to get a good degree, and to make the next paralympics, so everything has to be planned, and structured around the training. There are low moments, when your arms and legs won't work properly, or when it's another freezing morning on the track again, but I try to see the bigger picture. I'm 21, and I feel as if I'm living out every ounce of my potential. That's a good feeling.'

My day

'I get up around 7.30. Breakfast, thanks to my nutritionist, is healthy: porridge, or granola, tea. I don't drink, well the occasional glass if out with a friend, but never in the competition season, but I do have a good social life at Uni – you have to and not get too crazy with training, because it's all about balance, balance is everything.

During the day, it's lectures in the morning, from 9am until 2pm, study, library, friends. I'm always careful about what I eat, so lunch is meat or fish and lots of vegetables, and then at five, I drive myself over to the Athletics Centre, change into my kit and for the next two and a half hours, I train.

Each session, which runs for about two-and-a-half hours, begins with half an hour of warm ups, and then we have lots of different drills to go through to warm the muscles up to go into the main part session.

The running part takes me about an hour and a half, and then you have a warm down stretch, maybe a massage. My mother was amazing when I was young, driving me here five or six times a week, the sixty-mile round trip from Chepstow, after she'd done a day's work in her job as a civil servant. Now I can drive, it's easier.

It was disappointing to miss this year's World Games as I am ambitious, but every journey has its knocks and falls, and mostly I've been incredibly lucky not to have many injuries. My only real sacrifice is free time, but I'll get that when I have to stop running, and then my plan is to go into the grass roots of sport, I'm not sure as what yet, because at the moment I'm focused on making the team for the Rio Paralympics.

Spare time? Well, there isn't much. But I do love Cardiff, the city itself, and the contrast of going home to Chepstow and the family, where it's peaceful, lovely. I go out into the countryside and I jog around the local fields and pathways, and afterwards I feel so alive – it's a magical feeling.'

Press image Paralympics 2012

Jenny McLoughlin   127

Bettina Reeves

STAGE DESIGNER & PUPPET MAKER

When Bettina Reeves was 8 years old, her grandmother, the painter Dorothy Roberts, who had lived in China for twenty years, sent home eight sea trunks. They were stuffed with costume fabrics, silks, small clothes and 'sparkling things'. It proved the perfect magpie present for a child who was already making her own puppets and clothes.

Bettina (Tina to almost everyone) went on to study theatre design at The Camberwell School of Art, and later followed in her grandmother's footsteps by studying at the Slade.

After the Slade, this modest down-to-earth woman, achieved what felt like vertical take off: her first job was with the Young Vic in London, where she was assistant designer to John Macfarlane, now an international ballet and opera designer, and a lifelong friend. Next was the Royal Court where her first job, designing a Sam Shepherd play in which Bob Hoskins, and Kenneth Branagh appeared. It was daunting. 'I wasn't full of confidence then,' she says, 'but I was asked back.' Since then she's worked on countless West End shows and musicals and has a formidable reputation.

Marriage in 1976 led to a move to Molebutton Cottage in Govilon, once a derelict couple of cottages, which she and her husband restored, and where she had her children, Lucy 35, Will 32, and Tomos 26. She was in Brecon one day when she bumped into Joan Mills, who had recently become director of Theatre Powys, and who asked if she would work with her there.

HAVING WORKED ALL OVER ENGLAND, THINGS HAVE TO BE INTERESTING AND BIG TO ATTRACT ME BECAUSE THERE'S SO MUCH GOING ON LOCALLY

This chance meeting led to work with the Gwent Theatre, and for a few years she ran Gwent Young People's Theatre, where she put on plays by Shakespeare, Brecht, and Chaucer amongst others.

She moved to Abergavenny in 2001, and each year she runs an innovative installation workshop for the Abergavenny Food Festival. She produced amazing displays of huge animal puppets in 2012, which hung from the rafters of the grand Market Hall. The 2013 installation 'Gardens of Plenty', with its delicious looking velvet peas moving in the pod, is to feature on Countryfile.

Since 2000 she has worked as a lecturer in Theatre Design, mostly in Costume and Puppetry, at the highly-regarded Royal Welsh College of Music and Drama, recently voted by the Guardian as the top theatre school in the country. And it's here we meet, in Bute Park, behind the college's stunning new modernist building, where she is overseeing a puppet show put on by final year students.

The show was whacky, inventive, and stunningly costumed. For Tina, who watched impassively from the sidelines, it was the end of months of early mornings and late nights as every puppet was handmade and every stitch of costume purpose dyed in the vast hangar that is the students' prop room. At the end of the afternoon, this likeable, and quietly confident woman, looked as limp in repose as one of the puppets, but satisfied too.

Pass It On was the famous command from the teacher in Alan Bennett's play The History Boys – it being ideas, excitement, inspiration, professionalism. It's this ethos that runs through Tina Reeves life like letters through a stick of rock.

Personally self-effacing, she told us proudly that her daughter, Lucy, an actress and director, had recently appeared in her own sell-out, award-winning show at the Edinburgh Festival. Tina herself was designing a play at the Edinburgh Festival when she first discovered she was pregnant with Lucy. Lucy's great-grandmother, Dorothy Roberts, who became a well known artist in her own time, would have been pleased with the symmetry of that. The silk filled sea trunk from China passing it on.

My day

'My year falls into several parts: if it's term time at the Royal Welsh College of Music and Drama, I start at 7.30, and pretty much go through until 9.30 or 10.00 at night. I miss my garden during this time, and my singing, which I love with the Unicorn Singers.

There is always some price to pay, but I do love the work, and get a great kick out of seeing my students really sought out and making their mark as designers, both on the London stage and nationally. We do ten shows a year, and every four years take the show on the road – last year it was to Prague.

When term time ends, I'm usually pretty shattered, but I've always worked hard.

When we first moved here and when the children were young I freelanced locally. As the children grew older, I went further afield and worked all over England. One of my major challenges – at the time it felt like a major disaster – was designing the Hindu legend, Mahabharata. It had 200 people in it, loads of music, and we took it on the road all over England to Watford, Lincoln, Bedford. Being a community project, we sometimes performed in boarded up council estates, and sometimes in theatres. I was right out of my comfort zone, but I had to work having just got divorced, and in retrospect it taught me a lot.

Now, things have to be interesting and big to attract me because there is so much going on locally. I enjoy, for instance, making the huge puppet installations for the annual Abergavenny Food Fair, which has got bigger and bigger each year.

I still love the buzz of London, I could live there again. But what I love about living here are walking, doing my garden, wild swimming in the Usk and singing. Mostly though it's the incredible mix of local friends who keep me here. They're a broad cross section of playwrights, social workers, organic farmers, teachers, artists. I like that mix. It's never boring, but not too precious.

I think of myself now as a designer/maker and I'm looking forward to the next stage of my life, after college, when I can concentrate more on my own work, including drawing and painting, while enjoying the full life that living in the Borders has given me.'

Tiffany Murray

NOVELIST & LECTURER

YES, WE WORK
HARD, BUT NOT
NEW YORK HARD

'You'll find us behind two rusty jeeps and the house is a pig-sty, but don't worry about it.' The novelist and academic, Tiffany Murray, is directing us to her cottage.

Braced for a dump, we find a delightful Cider with Rosie type cottage perched on a vertiginous slope overlooking a place locally known as Little Russia. 'It's because they hardly ever get the sun,' says Tiffany, 'There's frost on their roofs until May.' The sound of birdsong is deafening on the day we meet, and down the steps we go, past her writing shed in the garden, into a low beamed 18th century cottage where coffee is brewing, the sun streams in, and the talk is fast and furious and funny. Tiffany is great company.

The kitchen was derelict when they moved in ten years ago. Home from New York, where she was a Fulbright scholar, Tiffany and her partner Larry, who runs his own antique lighting company, did it up bit by bit. Four years of spartan living, which meant no electricity, 'candles everywhere', no plumbing save for one outside pipe and loo.

Tiffany Murray is best known for her novels: Happy Accidents and Diamond Star Halo, both of which received great reviews, were short listed for the Wodehouse Bollinger Award, and widely translated. She's also the Dr. Tiffany Murray who warns, 'Don't ask for me in an emergency unless its related to Jean Rhys, or my work', and who teaches Creative Writing at the University of South Wales. A third hat arrived last year when she was appointed International Writing Fellow at the Hay Festival, a job which involves travel to the festival's offshoots – last year to India, Bangladesh, Nairobi, Spain,

Mexico, Budapest and Colombia to interview authors and talk about her own books. 'Yes, we work hard,' she agrees, pushing a plate of biscuits towards us. 'But not New York hard. The passion to write fuels what I do so it's a question of making enough money to clear time to make that happen.'

Her first two novels feature eccentric families, living in chaotic Arcadian settings, and both are coming of age stories written on the edge of England, where land 'spills into Wales'. She's been compared to Dodie Smith, Stella Gibbons and Kate Atkinson, but it's safe to say her own unconventional childhood is her strongest influence, particularly for Diamond Star Halo.

She was seven years old when her parents divorced, and her mother moved to the now famous Rockfield Studios on the outskirts of Monmouth, where Freddie Mercury and Queen recorded Night At the Opera, David Bowie produced Iggy Pop's Soldiers, and Oasis wrote and recorded Wonderwall.

'But before Rockfield, bands would stay at my mother's house on the Welsh border. It wasn't hers to be honest, it belonged to her boyfriend and it was a large old house, a vicarage. Musicians liked it because it had a big hall, great acoustics, and an easy atmosphere, and my mum is a great cook.'

At Rockfield it wasn't unusual for Tiffany to serve Freddie Mercury his supper. Queen recorded Bohemian Rhapsody there. Or she might barge in with a plate of sarnies while Motorhead were recording to tell the band, 'Mum says you've got to eat,' Tiffany says. 'As a very young child you're not interested in what people do. I didn't care that these people were famous musicians. What I remember most was the

LARRY AND I BOTH
HAVE SPELLS OF
MISSING NEW YORK,
BUT WE LOVE OUR
MORE GENTLE LIFE
HERE TOO

fun of it; lots of animals, lots of parties, lots of music, the other Rockfield kids, and this wonderful courtyard out the front where the stables were.'

A bohemian childhood was no bar to academic success. At London University, where she studied English and Drama, she graduated with a First Class degree. In 1993 she went to New York University on a Fulbright scholarship where she was a graduate student in Comparative Literature. She came home wanting to be a writer, and did another MA in Creative Writing at the University of East Anglia, which led to a PhD, an agent, and the writing of her first book, Happy Accidents, described as 'Woody Allen visits Cold Comfort Farm.'

Murray isn't a complete country turnip. 'Larry and I both have spells of missing New York,' she says, 'but we love our more gentle life here too – it's a place for getting things done. At the moment that means two very different novels out soon. First there's Sugar Hall, and again it's a novel on the Welsh border.

'The other novel is a Y.A. (Young Adult) – Renaissance, set in Florence, out in 2015. I had so much fun writing it and moving into a different genre to literary fiction. Finally there is a creative non-fiction book called Feast that has come out of my time as a Hay Festival fellow. Oh, and a film adaptation with novelist Owen Sheers, of my second novel Diamond Star Halo.'

My day

'On my ideal writing day, I get up at six, and write in longhand until I get hungry, and my dogs are nibbling my legs off for a walk. If I'm in Portugal, where my mother lives, I'll sit in the shade and usually write more because I can shut myself off from phones and internet, until her dogs start howling, nibbling, and need a walk.

In the afternoon, I have to do more physical exercise of some sort, and let's face it, when I say that I mean WALKING. It rarely gets more adventurous than this. Walking helps my head and I walk with a notebook and two large hounds. There are wild boar where I live, so I have to have one eye on the dogs and the other on my scrawls in my notepad. It can get messy. It's all forest here, so that's it: the forest and everything that lives in it.

I remember the writer Bernice Rubens saying to me, whenever you're stuck go for a walk. I owe a lot to Bernice because in the early days when I showed her my first short story in the back of a pub in Hay-on-Wye, she sat reading it, plumed in smoke, and eventually looked up, and said: 'Right, it's a mess, but there's something here.' It was the best encouragement I'd had.

THERE WILL ALWAYS
BE PANIC IN BEING A
WRITER – WHETHER
THIS IS FINANCIAL,
PROJECT-BASED, OR
LIFE-BASED

So afternoons, if I am home, are for exercise and pottering, and admin – which as any writer knows, means desperately trying to find other little jobs that just might pay. I teach a lot, and I enjoy it. I love working for the Arvon Foundation and for Tŷ Newydd on their residential weeks. I also do a fair amount of radio and I can rarely say no to a festival.

In the evening, often between five and seven, I'll sit and write randomly, wildly.

This is it – and the truth is sometimes I do this, and sometimes days are lost. There will always be panic in being a writer – whether this is financial, or project-based, or life-based (when do we say hello to other human beings?), or all of the above, to infinity.

But some days when I regret leaving New York, when I think I should be in a proper city, sucking life up, there is a moment when I'm grateful to be in this stone-walled cottage, in this place – for many reasons. But in the main it's tied to what I write: after growing up here and

returning and writing four novels based here, it's still a big mystery.

My cultural heartland is the Powys, Herefordshire border. It's where my mother's family come from; it's where I spent my childhood. I'd watch ponies on the hills around Hundred House; I'd spend days on my own, wading through the shallow River Eddw in the summer and coming home and playing the guitar very badly in my grandmother's garden.

If we left I'd miss the cut-off feeling. I'd miss the lack of clutter – the clutter of outside influences – as for the house I'm a terrible hoarder. I'd miss the silence of me and the page, although clearly it often drives me mad. You see, there's no procrastination with the silence of the forest around you, or if there is, you have to work damned hard at it.

The next few years will be very busy, but whether I'm working in Florence on the next few books, or teaching up in Shropshire or North Wales, I know that this shed on this hill is, for now, my writing space.'

Mary Rose Young

CERAMICIST & POTTER

Avoid the loose sheep as you drive through the Forest of Dean towards the studio of Mary Rose Young. Keep your eyes peeled too or you'll miss the low lying stone building that lies in the curve of a hill. It's only when you walk through the door that you'll find yourself in a potter's studio, which for sheer verve and invention, would not be out of place on the Left Bank, or in Manhattan, Madrid, or any of the artistic capitals of the world.

THE LIST OF HER FAMOUS COLLECTORS INCLUDES LADY GAGA AND OZZY OSBOURNE

If the very word pottery conjures up visions of worthy drinking vessels in various shades of mud, think again. This potter, from her bright pink hair to her lime green trousers, is drunk on colour and constantly experimenting, and each room in the house where she both lives and works gives the impression you have stepped into the pages of a slightly surreal children's book. The walls are painted in exuberant colour mixed with an artist's eye, bath and basins are enormous thrown pots, and from the ceilings hang a recent creation: the deliberately asymmetrical Alice in Wonderland chandeliers. The effect is so joyful and original that magazines from all over the world Elle, Interiors, The New York Times, have come to photograph her studio, and the list of her famous collectors including Lady Gaga, Ozzy Osbourne, and the late Nora Ephron, is constantly growing.

Mary Rose grew up in The Forest of Dean where she failed her eleven plus at a state primary in Lydney. Her father was a major in the army, and she spent a portion of her childhood travelling with him, 'like posh gypsies', first to a council house in Lydney, later to Spain where her parents ran a bar. In Spain, she met 'an exotic woman artist', who was drawing boats in the harbour. There and then, Mary Rose decided to become an artist.

After training at Cheltenham College of Art and Design, she set up her workshop in the Forest. In her first year of operation, 1986, she was accepted by the Chelsea Arts Fair, where she sold £3,000 worth of pots. The following year, she sold £10,000 worth. To date she has sold to thirty countries worldwide.

For seven years Mary Rose was a one woman band, until her big break came in the form of a commission from the uber fashionable Barney's, in Manhattan's Upper East Side. Liberty of London then took her on. When orders flooded in, she had to recruit more staff, and now has a work team of three to help her. Her brother James manages the business side of things.

Marriage in 1996 to Phil Butcher, a talented musician who once played bass for Iggy Pop, brought joy, and later a tragedy. Two years after their marriage, he went for a jog and had what she describes as a 'massive aneurism' and Phil calls 'a brain explosion'.

Mary Rose now looks after Phil, as well as designing and travelling extensively, to trade fairs and galleries where her work is exhibited. A sudden rush of inspiration during a recent rare holiday in Venice with Phil led her to paint a number of vivid watercolours of Venice, and of her home in the Border Country, which were exhibited last year at the Taurus Gallery, near Chepstow.

Asked to define the unique atmosphere of the Borders and Forest of Dean, she says: 'For me, it's simply home: the place where I am most myself, where I concentrate best. Lots of artists and writers live around here too, so it's a creative place to be without being pretentious.' Pretentiousness is something she abhors. Although collected by museums and galleries, she is a self-described 'artisan artist', and one who, for all her playfulness, is a grafter.

My day

'I get up at eight and go to the studio before my workmates appear. Then I go into my corner, think about what I'm going to do, and hopefully have a flash of inspiration. I work a straightforward nine to five day, and after work, I take Phil swimming, or we go shopping, to give him a bit of an outing.

As a potter, I could do all the work myself and put my prices up, but I like to make things that directly enhance life: objects you can use everyday. My aim, as much as possible, is to play – it's intoxicating, a bit like being drunk everyday – I like to make people smile.'

And it works. People do smile when they walk into this studio, they clap their hands and they buy, even though the pottery is not cheap, they want some of that magic before driving back into the forest again.'

Marian Voyce

BUTCHER

ALL SORTS COME
THROUGH MY DOOR,
SOME VERY HIGH
IN THE WORLD, AND
SOME JUST FRIENDS

Marian Voyce was married to Lionel Voyce, a man who did one thing well: he was a Master Butcher. 'He couldn't,' she jokes, 'change a plug, or put up a shelf, or paint a room.' But, show him a pig, and he could slice bacon by hand as fine as Chinese parchment; he could split a lamb with the delicacy of a surgeon; he understood the right length of time to hang beef.

For the forty nine years of their marriage, they worked side by side at their modest shop, FC Voyce, in Coleford. Meat-wise, he taught her everything she knew. She also did the books, and when he died, twelve years ago she was fully trained and determined to keep going.

The shop is now, in its own undramatic way, a local institution. Part social club, it has books you can read while you're waiting (or did until recently, when Health and Safety banned them). It has chairs to rest in, and you're always welcome to pop in for a chat, or cookery advice, which Marian dispenses in a gentle Gloucestershire burr.

'All sorts come through my door,' she says, 'some very high in the world, and some just friends. I'm very fond of my four widowers – all in their nineties. They come in and say, "So Marian, what shall I have for my tea tonight?" One of them lost his wife recently. He walked into the shop and I was thinking, poor old thing what will I say, when he announced: "I be come to tell you tha' I've got half a bed to let".'

Professional foodies as well as the broken-hearted beat a path to her door. She doesn't advertise, but when Matthew Fort, the Guardian's food writer, found her he gave her a full page rave. He admired her delicacy with her knife as she sliced her bacon by hand, the way she cross-hatched a piece of skirt across the vein, so it would cook easily and evenly.

Marian's particular too about continuing a family tradition that began in 1932, when Lionel's father delivered meat to the coal mines, everything must be traceable and local.

I'M GLAD I KEPT GOING – IT'S BEEN GOOD FOR MY HEART, AND MY HEAD

A true child of the forest, she was born and brought up in Yorkely Wood at a time when there was no television, no radio, and for amusement you went to Pillowell Wood with a bottle of pop and a packet of crisps, or to the local Methodist chapel three times on Sunday.

At Lydney Grammar school where she was educated, standards were uncompromising and high. She recalls a headmaster with a wooden leg who loved Shakespeare. If his pupils couldn't remember the lines, they were caned or severely reprimanded.

Her first job in a factory meant a fifteen-mile bike ride from home in Pillowell to the Lydney Industrial Estate. Pay £1.50 per week. After the birth of her son Paul in 1961, she carried on working, either in the shop or tending their garden in Cinderford where they grew all their own vegetables, and where she has lived for fifty five years.

While they were married, she and Lionel never took a holiday. She's made up for this since by travelling with three other widows to Malaysia, New York, Tenerife and Cuba. The poverty in Cuba reminded her of the Forest of Dean when she was growing up.

Work suits her: she looks bright-eyed, fit, a good ten years younger than her age, laughs a lot and says: 'I'm glad I kept going – it's been good for my heart, and my head.'

My day

'I'm up most mornings about six-fifteen. I leave the house around ten-to-seven to open up the shop and arrange the meat. We used to hang the carcasses in the window, nowadays it's jointed off the premises.

I'll have breakfast in the shop around eleven o'clock, and after that it's non stop all day. I'm either chopping meat, or ordering, or doing my books, or talking. It can get tiring standing up all day, so I'll jiggle my legs or do a little dance.

I close up about 5pm and no, I don't put my feet up – whatever gave you that idea? Mondays, I go to the gym, or I might go and visit my neighbours, or do some gardening, I've got a big garden. Or I might, if something has interested me during the day, get on the computer and Google things. I've got a paddock outside my garden so on Saturday, I get on my big mower and keep the grass down. A friend keeps sheep there so that helps.

Living here, well, it's my life. I know it all so well, the trees, the river, this town. I'd never think of living anywhere else.'

Annica
Neumuller

ABSTRACT PAINTER

**I'M DOING WHAT
I WAS ALWAYS
SUPPOSED TO DO**

When Annica Neumuller was nine, she drew a pastel abstract which her teacher framed and put behind glass. 'When she showed it to me, I felt joy. I remember it so clearly. I thought 'Great, I'm never going to die!'

Paris came next and self doubt. 'I'd stored that moment of triumph in my mind, I went there at nineteen and made attempts to paint with some "interesting" results. But I thought I can't do this, I'm deluding myself, and in effect, put away childish things and ended up studying Social Anthropology and History of Theatre at Stockholm University.'

In her late twenties, she got a 'proper job', working with refugees for six years. But it was back in Stockholm working with drug addicts, that Swedish-born Annica had another eureka moment. 'I was at an art therapy weekend, painting with some of the patients, when I thought that this is what I want to do.'

So it was back to Art School in Östersund on the Norweigan border from 1996-98, where this time she worked with fierce commitment – seven days a week and often seven nights – determined to slay the dragons of 'angst and self-doubt'.

It worked. She moved to Monmouth in 1999, and rented a house that was once a monks' Priory, close to St Mary's Church. It's set amongst grave stones and giant willow trees, and is wonderfully atmospheric, though not for the easily spooked.

The house is full of surreal and painterly touches: a dressmaker's dummy wound with feathers, a pair of red shoes on the floor, an exercise bike which she jokes is pure art installation. It's here, in a light studio overlooking the 11th century church, rebuilt in the 19th century, you'll find her, painting most of the day and much of the night.

Her strikingly abstract works are mainly exhibited at the New Leaf gallery in Monmouth where she recently had a hugely successful show, and in Abergavenny. Her paintings are in many private collections, including that of her agent, the late Jeremy Feathersone, a good friend and champion of her work. She is represented online by the prestigious Saachi Gallery, where she shows a large body of work. Annica also teaches stroke victims in art therapy groups.

'I'm doing what I was always supposed to do,' says this attractive, ebullient woman. 'It's not discipline, it's a compulsion: I have to paint every day otherwise I go mad.' Interestingly, Annica was extremely camera shy at the beginning of the photography session, but proved a fascinating subject once Alex helped her to relax.

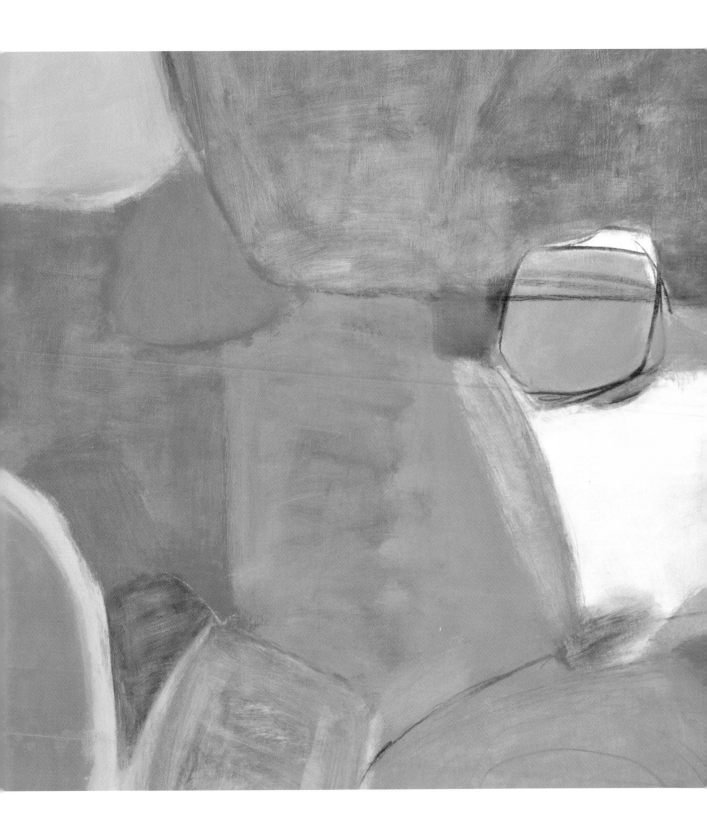

My day

'Etta, my dog and I, have morning coffee at Café Nero on Monnow Street. We sit outside on the pavement, and meet lots of local friends. When you live on your own, and work on your own, this contact is great – stops things getting too intense.

I'll paint for a couple of hours, and listen to lots of world music on the internet while I work. Break for lunch, walk again, work again. Am I boring you? It's not exhausting if you break it up, because I'm doing exactly what I want to do. Later in the day, I'll start work again, and then I go to the pub. If it's Wednesday to hear jazz at the Queen's Head nearby.

This is a beautiful place to live: I feel the presence of the monks in this house, and the hills and valleys around are perfect for walking Etta. At night I can hear the wind whistling in the trees, the choir practising in the church. The bell ringers, hmmm, an hour of them is lovely, but, every now and then, they'll practice for four hours which can drive me bonkers.'

BELL RINGERS
PRACTISING FOR
FOUR HOURS
CAN DRIVE YOU
BONKERS

Glenda Stoneman

ALPACA BREEDER

When Glenda Stoneman worked in a bank she wore four inch heels, painted nails and smart suits. Now it's wellies, overalls, and rubber gloves as she tends her expanding brood of twenty five alpacas, two hundred chickens and one dog.

The metamorphosis began in 2003, when she and her husband Peter bought ten acres of land, plus a house in Earlswood in South Wales. Both of them had lived in New York and London before and enjoyed busy professional careers, but a chance meeting with a 90-year old alpaca owner at the local Chepstow show changed everything.

'We were intrigued by this beautiful creature,' recalls Glenda. 'When we went home and did some research, we learned that they were full of character, easy to handle, light on the ground and, apart from being given water and hay, required little day to day handling.'

It was a light bulb moment for a couple wanting a change. They now run an eccentric but thriving boarding school for alpacas, as well as hatching and selling day old chicks, and eggs.

OH YES, WE HAVE LOTS
OF SEX ON THE FARM!

'We tend to organise alpaca births for the spring and summer and in a typical year we will have eight to ten births. It's the act of mating that encourages the female to ovulate, and she normally produces a single cria (baby alpaca) – twins are exceptionally rare. Male alpacas make a unique sound while mating known as orgling. It's a mix of a gargle and yodel, and the sound travels far, as one local farmer commented. During a programme for Channel 4, the producer asked me on camera if the alpaca and chicken breeding kept us busy. I said, without hesitation, oh yes, we have lots of sex on the farm!'

ORDER BOOKS
ARE SO FULL
THEY'RE USUALLY
SOLD BEFORE
THEY'RE HATCHED

My day

'My day, begins between 7.30 and 8am. If it's the breeding season, my first job is to check the baby alpacas. Alpacas originated in the Andes in Peru, and tend to be born between seven in the morning and midday, any later and they would freeze and die.

Occasionally, one will have got his head stuck through the fence, but mostly, they're low maintenance, resilient creatures. They're also excellent at scaring foxes away – they stamp and spit.

After I've fed the alpacas, I open up the chicken houses – we breed some lovely ones like Orphingtons and Light Sussex. Our chickens are popular because people know where the chickens come from, and that our standards of cleanliness are high. They can also phone us any time they want for advice, which means the phone rings all day! Between February and August, we put eighty eight eggs in the incubator; our order books are so full, they're usually sold before they're hatched.

Last summer, we also started chicken boarding so people can board their chickens when they go on holiday. Cleaning out the chicken runs can take up to an hour and a half, and then it's breakfast when Peter and I talk through jobs for the day: it could be haymaking, or teaching an alpaca to walk in a halter, or making the wooden chicken houses we sell.

If it's springtime, the alpacas are sheared. They yield about 3 kilos of fine fibre each, luxurious and soft. As the fibre is hollow, alpaca garments are cool in summer and warm in winter, so used for anything from fashion clothing to hard wearing walking socks.

It's a seven day, full on week. While I cook supper Peter's often answering emails, or catching up with paperwork. At eleven at night, I might be ironing or spinning wool from the alpacas. For Pete, the magical moments here are watching chickens being born – far more exciting to him now than making the big deals he used to at the bank. I like to stand outside at night and think that we've made this whole life for ourselves out of twenty acres of land. That makes me happy.'

CREDITS

Published by Graffeg 2014.
ISBN 9781909823082

Graffeg Limited
24 Stradey Park Business Centre,
Mwrwg Road, Llangennech,
Llanelli SA14 8YP
Tel. 01554 824000
www.graffeg.com

Graffeg are hereby identified
as the authors of this work in
accordance with section 77 of
the Copyrights, Designs and
Patents Act 1988.

Crossing Borders
Author Julia Gregson
Photographer Alex Pownall

Designed and produced by
Graffeg www.graffeg.com

Distributed by the Welsh Books
Council

**To the 21 women who have
told us their stories, our
warmest thanks.**